Building Family Friendly Ch

Building Family Friendly Churches

Mike Bossingham

inspire

British Library Cataloguing in Publication data

A catalogue record for this book is available
from the British Library

ISBN 1 85852 254 4

First published by Inspire
4 John Wesley Road
Werrington
Peterborough PE4 6ZP

Printed and bound in Great Britain by
Stanley L Hunt (Printers) Ltd, Rushden, Northants

Preface

O for a trumpet voice
On all the world to call,
To bid their hearts rejoice
In him who died for all!
For all my Lord was crucified,
For all, for all my Saviour died.

Charles Wesley (1707-88)

The gospel is for everyone, young and old, male and female, black and white, able-bodied and disabled, educated and uneducated and so on. I believe all these groups can come and meet together to worship God and to learn about him and about the power of the gospel. If I did not believe this I would not have used my precious sabbatical to write this book.

And yet this coming together so rarely happens. Most of our churches are representative of just one strand of society. There is a sort of apartheid going on as people of different cultures worship in different churches. In most of our traditional churches this is the culture of the middle class and mainly the elderly. In many ways, this makes relationships within a church simple as there is a mono-culture and less diversity of preference, but even where it does exist, it does not find expression in the church's worshipping life. It can be seen clearly that if everyone in a congregation likes a particular type of music or style of worship and preaching then it is a fairly easy thing for everyone to be content and for that congregation to be held together.

But are these the sort of churches we really want? Surely not, I hope. In fact, traditional churches will not survive unless they adapt themselves and appeal to a wider constituency.

The gospel challenges us to be welcoming and open to all: the elderly widow, the recently-retired couple, those with teenage children, those with young children, and single people of all ages. This is what I mean by 'family friendly'; a church that welcomes and meets the needs of all age groups and reflects the make-up of the community around it.

Throughout this book I am using the term 'family' to describe a multi-generational group of people with some kind of bond. This may be a family in the traditional sense of the word – mum, dad and their children – but will also include other patterns such as single-parent families, children brought to church by grandparents and so on. Ideally a church congregation should also be a family in this sense as it should be a multi-generational group with a common bond centred on Jesus.

One of the aims of this book is to encourage churches to become such families and be places where all ages can worship and learn together. This is much more challenging than the churches mentioned above, for in such a church there will be a range of tastes in music, style and formality and somehow all these differing needs have to be held together. I am amazed that Christian people, who preach tolerance and putting the needs of others before their own, can suddenly throw all this out of the window as soon as worship is mentioned. I am astonished that anyone can go to a church and expect everything on every Sunday to be to their personal taste. All age groups do this. The young person who wants modern worship every Sunday is just as guilty as the older person who always wants traditional worship.

For the most part, I have based my reasoning in this book on the observations that I have made as I have gone out and about, visiting churches that are exploring this route and talking to those involved. The theory is balanced with examples of all manner of churches up and down our country which are trying to be family friendly.

From all of this I have drafted the 'Family Friendly Charter' which gives churches that want to follow this route a statement of their intent. Coupled with this are resources listed and made available on the CD-ROM or the Family Friendly Churches Web Site. In addition there is a registration system so that you can be registered as a 'family friendly' church and be listed on the web site at www.familyfriendlychurches.org.uk.

A second aim of this book is to help churches become places that are inclusive and welcoming to all age groups, though the bias in what follows may seem to be towards families with children and young people. This is because I believe that a corrective has to be applied, since in the traditional churches the worshipping needs of younger people have largely been overlooked. In a sense the pendulum has to swing back a little the other way to correct for the attitudes and errors of the past.

Throughout this book I have adopted a couple of conventions. When talking about the work of individual ministers I use 'he' or 'she' as is appropriate to the gender of that minister. When talking about ministers in general I will use the plural 'they' to indicate that the minister might be either male or female.

The word 'minister' is used to describe church leaders in all denominations. In most cases it can be assumed to be synonymous with 'priest', 'vicar' or 'pastor'.

I use the word 'Sunday school' when talking about children's work that is run on Sunday, usually concurrent with the Sunday service. This does not mean that I believe this is what such work should be called. In fact, in my opinion it should be called anything except 'Sunday school'. I use it because it is a clear term that everyone understands.

Similarly I use the term 'midweek group' to indicate a children's group that meets midweek and includes an element of religious teaching. In reality these groups have a range of names.

Contents

1

The current situation

i) Where have all the children gone?

I used my sabbatical to write this book. During this time I celebrated my fiftieth birthday. I had been a minister for almost ten years. Before that I had been at college for three years after being a local preacher for two years. I had been preaching in total for around 16 years.

When I started preaching it was noticeable that in church after church, I preached to congregations where I was the youngest person present. When I observed this at the age of 40, it gave me some concern for the future. Now I am 50 I observe the same phenomenon. As I travel around my own circuit, in the vast majority of churches I am still the youngest person present. This no longer simply just concerns me; it makes me extremely worried about the future of the Methodist Church. What if, just what if, that is still the case when I celebrate my sixtieth birthday? And what will be there if, God willing, I manage to celebrate my seventieth?

So many Methodist churches, once full of children, are now like Hamelin after the Pied Piper has taken the children away. Even I can remember days when nearly all Methodist churches had active Sunday schools and attracted huge numbers of children Sunday by Sunday. Part of my journey to the ordained ministry involved leading a group of 20-30 or so 10-13 year olds in a large church in Bedford. Now the Sunday school has around that number of children in total – which in today's terms is doing well. My first contact with this church was helping to run a large open youth club; that club has closed, but the two smaller youth fellowship groups continue. The work continues, albeit on a smaller scale and in a more targeted style.

However, the bigger picture is very different. At the time when I was there work with young people was being done around the whole circuit. Now only the big town centre church continues with this work as many village chapels find themselves unable to continue any work with young people at all.

When I talk to older people in the circuit I now serve they reminisce about the old days, talking of youth groups of around 70 young people and Sunday schools of over 50 children. There are living memories, even in the villages, of huge numbers of young people attached to the churches. Photo archives exist of row upon row of children in the Sunday school and an army of young people gathered around a barbecue. Today the whole circuit musters a youth group of around half a dozen young people, and feels it is, and indeed is, doing well compared to the circuits around it, some of which are completely devoid of young people.

This is dramatically confirmed if you compare the fall in the number of children with us on Sundays, compared to the fall in the number of adults.[1]

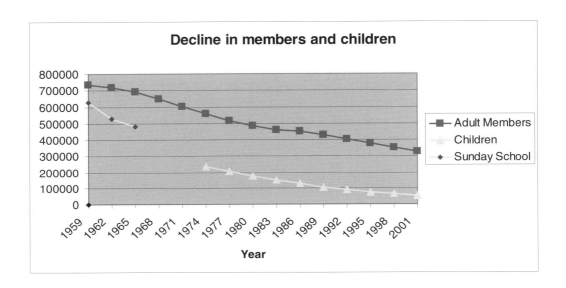

Even the mighty MAYC (Methodist Association of Youth Clubs) is a shadow of what it once was. I can remember going to the London Weekend as a young person and the numbers filled the Albert Hall – twice. Until 1995 the average attendance was 10,000 and there was a waiting list for those who hadn't bought their tickets early enough. The numbers have declined and the London Weekend could no longer pay

for itself, and so it was moved from the capital. Now 'Breakout', the successor to the London Weekend, caters for just 4,000 teenagers. A range of reasons has been given for this: the overall decline in church membership; the shrinking size of youth groups; and other events which attract young people's attention.

Overall, too, the number of young people has fallen.[2]

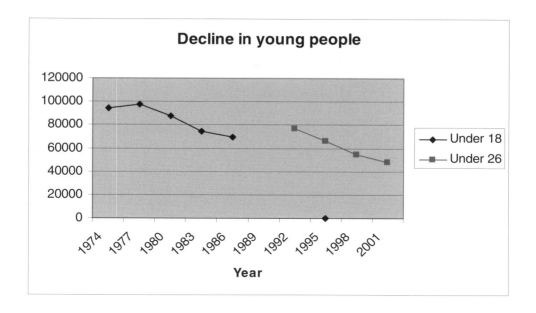

Decline in young people

Legend: Under 18, Under 26

The situation is similar, but not as drastic, with children. In many circuits there are churches doing good work with children. It is a different style of work to that of the past. In my circuit three of the village churches manage to run midweek children's clubs. These have replaced the traditional Sunday schools and are generally run in a more informal manner. One of these is working ecumenically with the Church of England. There have been many attempts to translate midweek attendance to Sunday attendance and this has proved to be largely impossible (except for Christmas all-age services and Mothering Sunday). Our experience is that parents are very supportive of the work and bring their children enthusiastically and regularly to these clubs, but it has proved impossible to get a level of involvement from them beyond this.

The two town centre churches in my circuit have managed to maintain Sunday schools (though they are not called that) running at the same time as the morning service, and one of them has seen this work expand quite dramatically in the last couple of years. Virtually all the children attending both Sunday schools are brought by their parents or grandparents, who then stay for worship themselves.

In very many ways there has been a shift from youth work to children's work. These days many youth clubs, which in the past would have served teenagers, are being run for children from 8-12. The figures for children's work in East Anglia show this shift quite clearly.[3] Note that most of these figures will be for midweek activity and that work with the over-13s has all but collapsed. The growth in midweek work has not impacted on Sunday attendance.

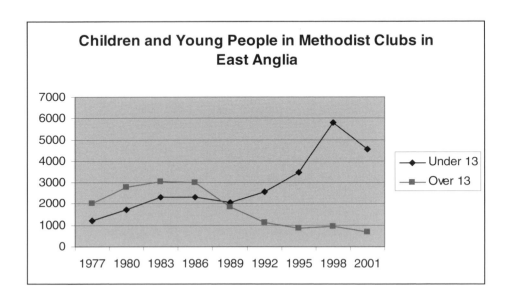

In all this it is safe to assume that around the whole circuit the days when parents brought children to Sunday school and left them there are over. Where Sunday attendance occurs, it is because parents bring their children and stay with them in church.

All this shows that overall we have seen a huge decline in the number of children and young people who are part of our churches. But the problem is not only in that age group, for their parents' generation is also largely missing. Our traditional churches have very few members in the 20-50 age groups.

The recent Church Life Profile[4] produced an age profile for the churches in general and then also for the Methodist Church. It can be seen that generally for the churches the age profile is higher than that for the country as a whole. This means that there are significantly fewer younger people (i.e. those under 50) attending church than in the general population. The figures for the Methodist Church are even more dramatic, showing even fewer young people attending Methodist churches than churches in general. The equivalent figures for the Church of England[5] show that many of these trends are echoed in this church too.

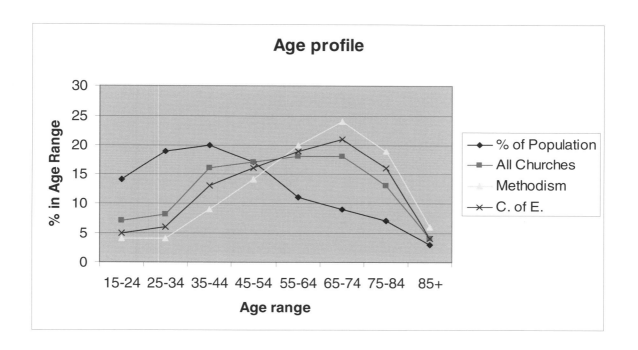

This profile inevitably means that the decline in church attendance will accelerate over the next few years. It is my estimate that unless we can reverse this trend the membership of the Methodist Church will halve again in the next 15 years.

There are a couple of well-known excuses for this lack of younger people in our churches. Some argue that the traditional form of church is a style that appeals to older people, and so as people get older they will come to faith and then start to come to their church. So, in a sense, there will be a constant supply of new elderly members who will keep the church going.

Oh, that this were true! Sadly, it does not appear to be happening, as very few people come to faith in later years. I remember holding a straw poll in a large Methodist church with a mainly elderly congregation. Out of a congregation of, I guess, around 200 people, only one of them had come to faith and started coming to church after their fiftieth birthday. If you don't believe me, hold a similar straw poll in your own church.

Another excuse for a church having no younger people is along the lines of 'We are in a retirement area here; there are no young people in our area.' I believe there is no such area in the United Kingdom. There are schools in every community, and in those schools are children and young people, and if there are children and young people in the schools, then nearby must be their parents. People have even said this of my home town – which has three huge secondary schools and countless primary schools. I doubt there is a single town or village in the UK that has no children or young people. What a congregation is doing here is projecting its own social make-up onto the community around it.

ii) The impact of all this

This absence of younger people is serious as I believe that it causes many of the problems that face traditional churches today.

As a minister I know how hard it is to find volunteers these days. I can remember the time when there used to be competition for an office and there had to be elections which could be hard fought. This is now a rarity. When an officer is needed today most meetings sit in an embarrassing silence waiting for someone to crack and offer to take the post.

In our larger churches, people tell me they are tired and it is the church work that is wearing them down. This is caused by two things. Firstly, they are at an age when they shouldn't have to be doing such things and, secondly, the level of professionalism required for many offices today is so high. Being treasurer is no longer just counting the collection and recording it in a book, but requires being familiar with Charity Law and being capable of completing the dreaded 'Schedule B'. A property steward needs to be aware of a whole raft of legislation including the Disability Discrimination Act and Health and Safety at Work.

In many of our village chapels the people who can deal with these issues just don't exist within the congregation. I have a village chapel in the Fens, where no one is of an age where they can be asked to hold office. They are desperate to keep their little church going, but don't have anyone to be the treasurer – and there is no one whom they can reasonably ask.

The reason for this is that the generation that once was the engine room of the church is missing, and in many cases a few of retired and elderly people are being asked to run a professional outfit.

At one time the minister would have helped out, but not any more, for we are desperately short of ministers. In my own circuit in 1993 there were three full-time itinerant ministers and then, in that year, for financial reasons, this was reduced to two ministers. This stretched the two remaining ministers to the limit. In the stationing round for 2002 we faced, for much of that year, the prospect of going down to just one minister for the whole circuit. Fortunately the Connexion appointed an excellent minister from

Nigeria at the last moment, but for a few weeks it felt as if we were looking into the abyss. This story is repeated over and over again around the Methodist Church in Britain, as each year there have been more circuits wanting ministers than there are ministers available.

We can see the decline in the number of ministers and local preachers since 1974 in the following graph.

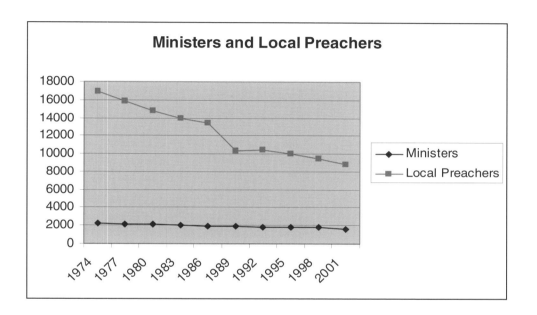

The number of ministers in full-time active ministry has fallen steadily from 2,210 in 1974 to 1,634 in 2001. Whilst the number of members and churches has also fallen, the number of schools, old people's homes etc. have not. This means that, although the church-based workload has fallen, (though with rising numbers of elderly members that could be disputed), the workload in the community has not declined and ministers can be very stretched. The dramatic fall in the number of local preachers is worrying and shows why the plan can be so hard to make these days.

Why such shortages? Disastrous changes in the selection and training of candidates are not the only reasons, neither is the deliberate reduction in training places, but, rather, the pool from which they would be drawn is largely missing in our churches. The church leadership says that it wants candidates in the 20-30 age range. But look around and you will find that this age group is hardly present in our churches. Is it any surprise that the age range of candidates has been rising when you look at the congregations from which they have to be drawn?

This shortage is compounded by the stress placed on those who remain. Too many of the people with whom I trained have left the ministry and many of those cited stress as the cause. I can understand that. I have seen the demands placed on me grow and grow as I try to paper over the cracks, and I have come close to breaking-point myself. In a sense this is resulting in a 'double whammy'. Not enough people are coming forward at one end and at the other end ministers are leaving.

Our financial problems also come about because we are top-heavy in membership. Many of our church members are now retired on fixed incomes and would perceive themselves as not very well off. I say 'perceive' because my experience of my parents and many of their contemporaries is that they are better off now than they have ever been. My parents can now easily afford luxuries, such as long-haul holidays, which they never could have afforded in previous years. This is not to deny that there actually is some great poverty among pensioners, but it would be very wrong to believe that being a pensioner and being poor are inevitably synonymous.

However, many churches have the perception that 'We are all poor pensioners here' and that will inevitably affect the amount given in the collection. This can be coupled with a lack of appreciation of the value of money these days and the level of giving needed to sustain the modern church. I know of cases where the amount placed weekly in the envelope doesn't even cover the cost of the envelope.

Shortage of finance is a real problem for the traditional churches. In my own circuit it has led to a reduction in the circuit staff and now just balancing the books is a major headache. Finding money for new initiatives is hard, and we are left trying to build the kingdom of God not on a shoestring, but on a broken shoestring budget. At the same time, in a sense, we are competing to get a message across against companies that have advertising budgets running to millions of pounds.

So it seems to me that the Church has three major problems: a difficulty in recruiting volunteers; an acute shortage of ministers; and a lack of finance. All these can be put down to the same cause, namely the shortage of people in the 20-50 age groups in our churches.

Our traditional churches are dying with their congregations so it seems that we are left with a difficult choice. We can offer our traditional churches 'palliative care' as they die and just provide support for each congregation until the numbers decline past the point of viability, and then one by one close our churches until there are no more left. I see many congregations that are dug in for this in what I call the 'This place should see me out' attitude.

Alternatively we can offer 'intensive care'. We can address the problems and work hard at changing churches and their culture so that they will attract these missing generations. We need to build churches that not only cater for children but also for their parents' generation, and so start to meet these problems head-on.

My suspicion is that in the medical profession you cannot do both simultaneously and for churches, too, we have to make a choice. Either we can cradle individuals while their churches close, or we can fight to change the churches to keep them open and active.

My preference is clearly for the latter. This book is exploring a way of trying to do just that. But first let us explore how we have got into this mess.

iii) Why have all the children gone?

Up and down this country are thousands of Sunday school teachers and youth club leaders who have given years and years of committed and hard service, have seen hundreds of children go through their hands and yet have seen barely any of them become committed Christians in their own denomination. Those who have stayed in the Church have drifted towards the newer churches meeting in school halls and homes. I am occasionally asked to preach in such churches and am always taken aback by the number of people who come up and tell me they went to a Methodist Sunday school or youth club.

These, though, are the minority. Undoubtedly the vast majority of them are still impacted by the teaching they have received. They do believe in God and some version of the Christian creed and they are in sympathy with the Church, particularly the one in which they grew up. I used to meet this particularly in a church that had a strong Boys' Brigade. There were countless men over the years who had a love and sympathy for that church and expressed it in all sorts of ways, except the one that mattered. This sympathy did not extend to becoming active worshipping members of that congregation. They perceive the worship of the church to be simply irrelevant to their lives.

How has this come about? I believe it is because that there was not a unified approach to the Christian development of these children and young men and women. Generally children and young people were separated from the main church in their Sunday schools and youth clubs. In these they were permitted to worship, if they worshipped at all, in a contemporary manner. They tended to seek a less formal style of worship and a different type of church music. Whilst this happened in its own setting then everyone was happy, but as soon as they tried to bring this informality and music into even a part of the main worship of the church they were fiercely opposed. This still happens today.

The best way I can illustrate this is to talk about my own experience in a youth group called the 'Pacesetters'. In the late 60s and early 70s I belonged to a typical teenage group of 15-20 young people. We met in a Methodist church in Cornwall even though a number of us went to the local Church of England church. In this large rambling building we had been allocated exclusive use of a room and had decorated it ourselves. It had a slatted ceiling and a low, wide bench all the way round that was covered with foam and then fur fabric, which then also ran to about half-way up the walls. The church was really tolerant and even allowed us to smoke there!

Here we would sit in our own room, smoking and discussing the issues of the day, led by a saintly man called Bill Cheshire. At times a guitar would be produced and we would sing some of the trendy modern songs, like 'Kum ba ya' and 'Lord of the Dance'. I guess countless teenage groups were doing roughly the same thing in churches up and down the country.

Looking back on the situation I now realise that the tolerance had its limits. We could do whatever we wanted in our room, but that was it. When we wanted to lead worship and bring the sort of worship we had discovered and liked into the church, even once in a while, then the tolerance disappeared very rapidly. I still remember the battles – 'You cannot do this'; 'You cannot sing that'; 'Guitars – devil's instruments'; 'That will upset Mrs Jones' and so on.

I have managed to track down some of the ex-Pacesetters and gathered their views. Remember that these comments are not coming from teenagers, but from people now in their late forties and early fifties:

> 'I don't always get that much out of the service. I am sure that that is partly due to my sitting on the fence, but also, services can be uninspiring.

> I also find that the church seems to be preoccupied with raising money all the time to keep itself going.'

> 'Graeme always supported me in encouraging the children's involvement in the past and attends church on an occasional basis now, as well as belonging to the men's evening fellowship/supper group, but is no nearer faith now than he was when I married him.'

> 'I am on the electoral roll of our parish church, although my involvement with the church is small; Anna is a member of the choir and my visits to church tend to be in support of specific events or on high days and holidays. Both our children, Helen and John, went to Sunday school and are confirmed members of the Church of England. Helen has a strong faith but does not regularly attend any church, John, I don't know, but at 17 it is certainly not high on his list of priorities.'

I am sure that other groups from later times can add their own stories to these; for instance, the refusal of churches and organists to play songs like 'Shine, Jesus, Shine' when they were published. I once witnessed an Anglican priest who had to read the words aloud because the organist refused to play the music. This was compounded by the inability of many congregations to accept a slightly more informal style and the reluctance of congregations to modernise their buildings and to start making use of new technology, even, in some cases, a simple OHP. It is this overall refusal to listen, respond and partially adapt to meet the worshipping tastes of the following generation that has driven this generation out of the traditional churches.

I know of churches that still pride themselves on the fact that they have kept out these modern songs, modern informal styles, and projectors and screens without realising that the very thing they are proud of is killing their church.

In my visits to churches I experienced a baptism at Burbage Methodist Church. After the baptism the minister, Ken Hawkins, showed the baby to the congregation. As he did so he said these words:

> May this church grow strong with love and joy, contentment, purpose and sacrifice, that Kathryn Louise and all our children may learn the way of Christ and of servanthood. This is the challenge we are all about, to nurture young lives in love, to bring her life to the experience you seek; contentment and fullness in the grace of our God and Jesus Christ, crucified and present in our lives.

It is the duty of each generation to nurture the next one in the faith, the knowledge and love of Jesus Christ and help them in the task of searching for, and building, a way of being church that supports their task. This is something a church promises at every baptism, yet I believe that it is a promise that has not been kept neither for my own generation nor for the succeeding generations. It is this failure that this book seeks to address.

iv) Splitting families up

But there is another problem today. The whole way we do church tends to divide families rather than bring them together. Our way of functioning as a church does not meet the needs and aspirations of modern families.

When I was a child, in common with many other children, I was packed off to Sunday school in the company of my little sister. My parents didn't come to the church, so my suspicion is that they wanted a bit of peace and quiet on a Sunday morning and the local church was as good as any other place for us to go. I suspect many other parents on the estate felt the same, for it was a busy little Sunday school meeting in a green corrugated hut. I expect that they had seen quite enough of us during the week and this was a welcome break.

This was a pattern that suited the lifestyle of the 1950s and modern churches have inherited this pattern. It is a pattern of dividing up families.

On Sunday mornings, in those churches that still have children, they troop out for

Sunday school, normally after around 15 minutes. Perhaps there is a group for them midweek and possibly a uniformed organisation too. There might be a youth club on a Friday evening. All these activities split them from the other members of the family, and, because they are most likely of different ages, split them also from their siblings.

Their mother may well go to a women's group. It is unlikely to be an afternoon fellowship group as nearly all of these are timed to coincide with work and/or school pick-up time (and then such groups often wonder why they cannot attract younger women), so her group is much more likely to be during an evening. Perhaps she will work on the flower rota, involving a commitment probably on a Saturday afternoon. She may also be part of the catering committee so that even when there is an event for all ages at church, she is not part of it as she is stuck in the kitchen.

Then there is their father. He may serve on the property committee, not only going to meetings (usually in the evening), but then going along with his toolkit to do odd-jobs around the church. Then, perhaps there is a men's fellowship or a house group of which he is a part. Of course, in these days the roles may well be reversed, but the impact is the same.

Each person in the family has their own activities on different nights and when one is in the others are out and vice versa. Often the family is rarely together, because of work coupled with church commitments. This cannot be healthy for families. I have heard teenagers complain that they never see their parents because they are always out at church meetings. Ask yourself how this can all work in a single-parent family! If you want to see an extreme version of this situation then just take a look in a manse with a family or, even worse, a manse where both parents are ministers!

If you think this isn't true, I challenge you to look at your own church and ask this key question: 'Does my church offer anything, on a regular basis, to families that they can do together?' I would be very surprised if there were many that did, unless the parents are leading the activities the children are doing, but that isn't really what I am talking about here.

Lifestyles have changed since my parents packed us off to Sunday school in the 1950s. These days, in many households, not only do both parents work, but they have high pressure jobs that take a lot out of them. It seems as if companies have to be led kicking and screaming to make employment 'family friendly'. Companies may pay lip-service to the ideals, but the pressures on the shop-floor can be very intense. Many parents work long hours and then have long journeys at the end of the day. Travel to and from work takes much longer and can be more stressful.

It may be that someone else collects the children from school and keeps an eye on them until a parent can pick them up. It may even be that this person gives them their evening meal. In many households breakfast is eaten 'on the hoof'. If both of these are happening then it can easily be seen that a family doesn't eat together at all in the week.

It is not only parents who are stressed, for children are too. When I was young I can just about remember the Eleven Plus. I can remember passing, but I cannot remember taking it as it was done in such a low-key manner. I didn't then have external exams again until GCEs at the age of 16 and then A levels at the age of 18. And that was it.

Contrast that with children today. They take SATs in years 3 and 6 and then again in year 9, and then GCSEs in year 11, ASs in year 12 and then A2s in 13. All these are external exams and great pressure is applied on them as well. For example: SATs, which were originally designed to assess teachers, are portrayed to children as important, and year 6 children are often told that their streaming at secondary school will be based on their SAT results. As if that wasn't bad enough, today a vast amount of course work is also assessed and becomes part of the overall mark. So nearly every piece of work is almost like a mini-exam. No wonder our children are stressed out and often have little time for outside interests, including church and worship.

I have had parents say to me, when their children reach year 10 and start their GCSE courses, that they can no longer be part of the church, or youth fellowship, because now they must focus on their school work. I can understand why parents would want to do that, but it takes young people out of the church at a crucial stage

in their spiritual development and many will never pick up that search again later in life.

Patterns of entertainment have changed too. Our family did not have a television when I was a child. We often spent our evenings playing games together, pursuing hobbies and listening to the radio. Even when occupied with different interests we were doing it together. That togetherness applied even in households that had a television, for there was one television, and the watching of it was a communal experience. Bedrooms were for sleeping in because they were too cold to spend any time there.

Contrast that with today. Most children have several forms of entertainment in their bedrooms. Many have their own television and probably a computer too, perhaps even with internet access. Being sent to their bedroom is no longer a punishment for a child. I remember learning that the hard way when our children were little. After the 30 minutes' 'punishment' we shouted up the stairs: 'You can come down now' to be greeted with the response: 'Thank you, but we'd rather stay up here.'

With all these factors families rarely spend time together, not even mealtimes. We insist in our household that we sit around the table together for the evening meal. We even insist that members of the family do not answer telephones (two landlines and four mobiles!) during this shared mealtime. In a two-minister household that is really difficult to do, but we insist on it, and, anyway, the answering machines will take the messages. We believe that in having this uninterrupted family time we are the exception, rather than the rule.

All of these factors mean that a modern family spends very little time together and therefore doesn't want a church that will split them up. I recently came across a family in which the parents work together running a local post office, newsagent's and convenience store. They work very long hours for six and a half days a week. They are in sympathy with the church and its ideals and are quite happy to send the children to a holiday club. But they want to be together, not split apart in their precious time off together and in addition they want it to be enjoyable and fun. Other families echo this sentiment.

All of the above applies to families where the parents are living together, but there are those who, for one reason or another, live apart. Here pressures can be even greater. Sunday is a popular day for access when the estranged parent can meet his or her children. This time together is extremely precious. Is such a parent really going to want to sit in a church while the children troop out into a Sunday school?

How can we cater for families who feel like this? Can we find activities that they like doing together? Does it have to be on a Sunday morning? If so, what shape of service will suit?

The modern challenge is to find ways of doing church that keep families together and makes the time spent in this way valuable and 'family friendly'. It is not easy to go from where most churches are at the moment to a church that meets the needs of the families described above.

v) A divine responsibility

But more than this, I believe too that our way of functioning as church does not meet with God's ideal for it. The concept of community, and particularly the community as expressed by family, echoes the Godhead itself. Key verses here are Genesis 1.26-27:

> Then God said, 'Let us make humankind in our image, according to our likeness; and let them have dominion over the fish of the sea, and over the birds of the air, and over the cattle, and over all the wild animals of the earth, and over every creeping thing that creeps upon the earth.' So God created humankind in his image, in the image of God he created them; male and female he created them.

The first point to make is that God here is addressing himself in the plural form, 'Let us make ...'. Here is a picture of God, not as a lone figure, but much rather as a member of a community. This may be an image of the heavenly court community or a hint of polytheism creeping into the text. Christians would like this to be the Trinity and, although commentators on the whole feel this is unlikely, echoes of the Trinity can be seen in the creation process.

Genesis 1.2 can be translated as 'the spirit of God was hovering over the waters'. Proverbs 8.22-30 and John 1.1-3 both give us imagery of the Christ figure being present and instrumental in the creation. There may be differences in how we see that community, but there can be no doubt that this verse and others define the Godhead as a close community or family.

This God then makes humankind and we are told, 'male and female he created them'. As male and female we are made in the image of God. The image of God cannot be seen in man alone, nor in woman, but rather in the wholeness of humanity. God, who is a community, creates man and woman to be in God's image when they are in community with each other.

God is beyond gender which, as an aside, makes one wonder why female imagery for God should still be a contentious issue for some. More importantly for this book is that the idea of God as a family promotes marriage and family life, not only as something that is ordained by God, but as something that is in the likeness of the Godhead itself. When churches turn away or fail to cater for families, they are rejecting entities that bear the image of the creator themselves. This concept is echoed by Ephesians 3.14-15:

> For this reason I bow my knees before the Father, from whom every family in heaven and on earth takes its name.

Here we see an idea that the very concept of family itself is rooted in God.

God is a divine family and this is expressed in how he relates to us. God is the creator of all family groupings and their existence and significance are dependent on him. The Bible reveals this aspect of God's nature in a rich and varied use of family imagery: God is our Father, God is husband to his people, God is like a nurturing mother, Christ is the bridegroom of the Church.

When a man and a woman come together in marriage, God gives to them something of his own being, the concept of being family. A human family – man woman, children – live up to the true meaning of family as they try to reflect the source of their family life, the Godhead itself.

This is a huge calling and responsibility and one that the Church needs to help families to live up to. A church, too, reflects something of the Godhead when it truly echoes these qualities of family. Yet how can we do this, when so many churches regard children as a nuisance rather than part of something that reflects the divine?

One generation has a God-given duty to teach the next the words and ways of God. Over and over again in the Old Testament there are passages like Deuteronomy 11.19:

> Teach them to your children, talking about them when you are at home and when you are away, when you lie down and when you rise.

Even the Passover meal has a teaching element. The youngest child is included and involved in the celebration as he or she asks: 'Why is this night different from all other nights?' The following words and action are there to allow the children and others to understand and experience the liberation that was won for them by God.

If this passing on does not happen and a new generation grows up ignorant of God and his ways (as appears to have happened), then it is not the fault of that generation, but of the one before. They have failed in their God-given role to teach the next generation.

When I baptise children I worry sometimes about the promises that the parents make and whether they have a serious intention of keeping them. However, I worry just as much about the members of the congregation as they make their promise.

> Members of the body of Christ, we rejoice that these, our sisters and brothers, have been baptized. Will you so maintain the Church's life of worship and service that they may grow in grace and in the knowledge and love of God and of his Son Jesus Christ our Lord?[6]

The phrasing is clear, the purpose of the Church's life of worship and service is so that the next generation may grow in grace and in the knowledge and love of God and of his Son, Jesus Christ our Lord. Is that the purpose of most churches today? How many congregations can answer that with a clear conscience? Or are they, as I suspect in far too many cases, serving exclusively the needs of the older generation at the cost of the rising generation? Far too often the baptism takes place outside the main congregation and they are not even there to make the promise! How far the people of God have fallen, that they are not even present when a new little one is accepted by God in baptism.

Jesus has even stronger words concerning children, as in Matthew 18.2-6:

> He called a child, whom he put among them, and said, 'Truly I tell you, unless you change and become like children, you will never enter the kingdom of heaven. Whoever becomes humble like this child is the greatest in the kingdom of heaven. Whoever welcomes one such child in my name welcomes me. If any of you put a stumbling-block before one of these little ones who believe in me, it would be better for you if a great millstone were fastened around your neck and you were drowned in the depth of the sea.'

The disciples have been arguing about greatness. Jesus brings a child into their midst and sets him or her before them as an example. Unless you become like this child, he says, with a child's humility and indifference to power and status, you cannot enter the kingdom of heaven. Children in churches are not just sponges to sit quietly and absorb everything they are fed, but also they are there to have their own insights and to make their own contribution. Sometimes the wisest words and greatest insights come from children, and adults would do well to listen and encourage such contributions.

So often adults see children as 'the church of tomorrow'. That perception is so limited and limiting. They are part of the church of today and should be able to play an active part in it. Jesus says we should be able to learn and draw from their insights.

In terms of the future, they are still not simply 'the church of tomorrow', but much more the leadership of the church tomorrow and consequently the most valuable resource the church has. I have come across some churches, fortunate to have children, who expect the children's work to be funded from the pennies the children bring themselves. Can that be called investing in the future? How many churches are really, and I mean really, investing in this resource?

Jesus says that they are much more than a group of little people at the front. Welcome a child and you welcome Jesus into your church. Just imagine that the two year old who is stampeding around your church is really Jesus in disguise. Think about that before you have a go at his or her parents. If the two year old Jesus was really running around in your church would you really say to Mary, 'You are only welcome here if he behaves himself better than this.'

Finally, some of Jesus's most stern remarks are directed to those who would put a stumbling-block before a little one. Are not those who expect church to be purely an adult experience dangerously close to that?

It is my feeling that many traditional churches have fallen a long way from the places God would have them be. Although some traditional churches work hard to be such places, still many are not places that reflect the image of God in terms of being a family and welcoming families. Too many churches are not places where children are welcomed and taught the faith. Too many are not places were young people are encouraged, valued and nurtured. Too many are not places where the image of Jesus is seen in the 'little ones'. Too many have been too often places where children and young people find faith despite the church rather than because of it.

This is a major factor in the decline of the traditional mainstream churches. I believe that is so, not only because they do not nurture young people for the future (and common sense says that will happen to any organisation that fails in this way), but also because God wills it. God wants all our churches to be places where all, including children and young people, are welcomed, taught and nurtured. But so many of our churches are so far from this model (a model that echoes God himself) that he simply cannot bless them and help them to grow.

There is a huge task ahead, but my experience has been that when a church reviews itself and sets about the task of becoming the sort of church God wants it to be, then very rapidly he will bless it and it will see fruit and growth once more.

vi) Conclusion

I believe that we have largely failed to bring the countless children and young people from our Sunday schools and youth ministry into our adult congregations for the following reasons:

1. We have failed to be the sort of open and welcoming churches to families that God wants us to be.

2. There has been a lack of joined-up thinking for at least my lifetime. Children's and young people's ministry has been done in isolation from the rest of the life of the church and particularly from the worshipping life of the church.

3. We have largely failed to reform worship so that it is, at least in part, relevant and satisfying to the rising generations.

4. We have stuck with old patterns of dividing up families rather than bringing them together in the life of the church. The traditional churches have one last chance. We can rise to these challenges and establish a future for ourselves or we can continue in the same old ways and one by one close our churches. This book sets out a way of implementing the kind of reforms that are required.

2

Churches that buck the trend

During my sabbatical I visited a number of very different churches around the country, but they all had one thing in common: they were working towards being family friendly and were seeing some growth as a result.

I visited both Anglican and Methodist churches, both large town centre churches and small rural churches, and churches with both new and traditional premises. Details of these churches can be found on the CD-ROM that accompanies this book.

I added these visits to my own 25 years' experience of working with children, young people and families. This chapter is a drawing together of these experiences.

There were largely ten clear factors that these churches had in common.

1) There was an individual or small group with a heart and a vision for work with children and families. It was very noticeable in the churches I visited that there is a clearly identifiable individual who has been at the heart of the changes. In a few cases, usually the larger Methodist churches, this person was the minister of the church. This seemed to happen where the church was the largest or only church in the minister's charge.

In the smaller Methodist churches the individual with the vision for change was generally a lay person and a member of the church. They had managed to obtain the support of the minister, along with the Superintendent of the circuit, but it was the lay people who had brought the process forward.

In the Anglican churches I visited, it was the parish priest who recognised the problem and then approached specific lay individuals to find ways of addressing the situation.

2) This group or individual had managed to share their vision with most of the rest of the church. This was done by gentle but persistent persuasion. The changes hadn't happened straight away and the individual had taken a few knocks along the way, but they continued on regardless. In the end it was noticeable in some churches that those who opposed most vehemently became the greatest supporters when the ideas were seen to work.

In some cases the changes happened slowly. At Burbage new songs were introduced in the time before the main service and then some four or five years later incorporated into the services.

Fleggburgh spent some 18 months researching, training and planning for the changes. Other churches took time visiting other churches and examining what they were doing. This was particularly true of Elburton.

Some churches like Heartsease Lane had a bad experience in the past. There they lost a whole number of families because of their unwillingness to change, so when the present minister started the process of change again they were much more accepting of the changes, as they knew at first-hand the risks of not changing to accommodate families.

In other cases it was the closing of an existing Sunday school that spurred a church into action and helped to pave the way for new work to begin.

3) Reform of the church's worship to make it family friendly was seen as an absolute priority. In every case changes to worship were at the heart of the process. The point has been made and will be made many times in this book that it is not enough to cater for children and young people during the week. These churches saw it as not enough to cater for children, young people and families in this way (though they have midweek activities), but have made the changes to their main act of worship so that its appeal can be broadened. This was an absolute priority for many of the churches and particularly the parish church at Wiveton.

Some did this by working on the time (usually at the beginning of the service) before the children go out and widening the appeal of this time – and quite often its length. Others moved to all-age worship on every Sunday and others have organised a second service alongside their main service. This second service may be in the church hall, parish rooms or even a school hall. Some mixed a combination of these ideas, perhaps doing different things on different Sundays or running a more informal service in the hall which itself has a Sunday school.

However, where the changes were implemented the churches realised that the worship had to be changed from traditional patterns for growth in these areas to occur.

4) The church council, recognising this, discussed calmly and openly the changes that needed to be made to the worshipping life of the church. How they worship is very important to people and passions can arise in such discussions, people can feel threatened and meetings can become very heated.

However, an important first step for these church councils was to recognise that there really is a problem for churches today and that their worship had to change if they were to address the difficulties.

The churches that succeeded here are those which were able to face up to the problems described in the last chapter, discussed this calmly, and then developed a pattern of worship that has something relevant for each generation.

These churches also consulted widely, not only talking about the changes themselves, but also discussing them with the church hierarchies, local preachers' meeting, the Superintendent Minister etc.

5) There has been openness to new and creative patterns of worship. These churches were open to new ideas and have encouraged creativity. They did not restrict themselves to one style of worship, but the churches concerned were willing to give a range of styles a try, review them and then make any adjustments that were required. No church got the changes right first time and so this process of change, review and adjust was really important.

There are in most churches people who demand that worship does not change and that it should suit them every week. However, the churches that have become family friendly seemed either to have very low numbers of such people or else had managed to persuade them of the need for change.

It was noticeable that the vast majority of churches made use of projection and used it creatively, not just for the words of hymns. In addition a sizeable minority took advantage of data projection. Whether projection was available or not much use was made of visual aids.

Most of the churches also supplemented the use of the organ with other instruments and a sizeable minority (and particularly those running concurrent acts of worship) did not use an organ at all. Some used a piano or a keyboard alone, but often a number of musicians played together in an ensemble. This would often include a piano or keyboard, which would then perhaps be coupled with guitars and a range of more traditional instruments, such as flutes, violins, cellos, clarinets, saxophones and so on. Churches had used great imagination in building a group from the available musicians.

In all cases the worship was less formal than traditional worship. The congregation was often invited to participate in, and respond to, the worship and teaching. In some cases the style could truly be called interactive. The services were conducted with a light touch and a lack of formality which created an overall atmosphere of gentle good humour.

None of the churches had completely thrown away the traditional elements of worship, but were doing their best to maintain a balance between the old and the new.

The exceptions were the churches that opted for multiplexing and held separate services in, usually, the church and hall. It was interesting to note that in these churches joint worship of the two congregations was unpopular with just about everyone.

6) There was willingness amongst lay people to take a responsibility for worship and to lead part of the Sunday worship. This was very noticeable in all the case study churches. In all cases part of the worship was led by a lay person or a rota of lay people from the host church and this was usually the part of the service where the children were present.

Usually there was a time of worship using adult worship songs which were accessible to children, and in some cases children's songs were used. This was generally followed by an introduction to the theme and again this was often geared towards children. There was evidence of a high level of co-operation between these lay worship leaders and the preachers appointed to lead the service. This was often achieved by using either the lectionary readings and themes or using material that has its own scheme, such as SALT (a scheme of weekly children's and all-age material published by the Scripture Union).

London Rd in King's Lynn stood alone in encouraging teenagers to lead the worship for their peers – this has led to two 16 year olds to start training as preachers.

7) The appropriate authorities were consulted and gave their support. The ideas were discussed with the appropriate church authorities and were supported by the authorities.

In Methodist terms, the appointed preachers were willing to stand aside and let lay people lead part of the worship. In some cases they were willing to use the material suggested by the church and preach on the themes given in this material. Circuit Superintendents were especially supportive and some were willing to plan to the church only preachers who would co-operate with such a scheme.

In Anglican terms, vicars or priests in charge were also willing to stand aside to support and encourage lay people to lead worship.

'The Bridge' at Burbage also consulted the local community using a survey to solicit viewpoints from the doorstep.

8) In most of the case studies the lay people who were leading this part of worship were willing to undergo some training for undertaking this task. A key to the success of these schemes was the willingness of the lay people leading worship to undergo training for their new ministry.

There were essentially two types of training used. Some preferred to use courses geared towards children's work (such as *Kaleidoscope*[1]) and others preferred training courses for leading worship (such as the Methodist Worship Leader's Course[2]).

A good example of this was at Fleggburgh, a tiny Norfolk chapel, where five out of the seven members took *Kaleidoscope*[3] training before any decisions were made about the future.

9) The changes in most case studies were small, but consistent Sunday by Sunday. All the churches ensured that at least part of their worship was family friendly every Sunday so that there was consistency week by week.

In most cases small changes were made, were reviewed and further small changes made. It seemed that, generally, there had been a progression of small changes rather than one huge change.

'The Bridge', for example, attracted many more unaccompanied children than originally expected and adjustments had to be made, and at Heartsease Lane the children's work was changed dramatically when conduct became a problem.

10) All the churches saw some growth in the numbers of children, young people and families worshipping with them. This was the pay off. In all cases families started to return to Sunday morning worship surprisingly quickly. My experience at London Rd, King's Lynn, supports this. Here I introduced a family friendly element to the morning worship when I was present (about one week in three) and this was enough to start to draw children and families back into worship within a few months. This was also true of Fleggburgh, where children and parents were worshipping at the church within weeks of the church's implementation of its plans for family friendly worship.

It was also very noticeable that families were willing to travel some distance to find suitable churches. This was very much the case at Blackshaw Head, a village church that had reversed the normal flow; here families drove from the local towns to worship in this tiny village church.

All the churches had the full range of ages present and the style of worship reflected the breadth of ages represented. There was a high degree of tolerance of small children for it was very noticeable that many of these churches accommodated not only children, but also adults with special needs.

3

Models of family friendly worship

My experience is that very modest changes will make a huge difference. I believe there are three models that can be adopted and these are listed further down in this chapter.

However, these models are not mutually exclusive. They can be combined and used in an overall strategy. The combination can either be in terms of time, that is, doing different things on different Sundays, such as having a main service and Sunday school on three Sundays a month and an all-age service on the fourth Sunday; or the combination can be in terms of space, multiplexing (the term comes from cinemas that offer a wide selection by having many screens) in two rooms, one having a traditional service and the other an all-age service; or a church combined with a Sunday school.

Some of the churches I visited managed to have a strategy that combined all three models. The case studies describing the churches I visited whilst researching this book can be found on the CD-ROM. These will be helpful as they describe a wide range of church styles and approaches.

i) Main service combined with Sunday school

This is the most traditional approach, though actually you don't have to go too far back to discover that traditionally Sunday schools were run at a different time to the main service. Generally the children stay in worship for around 15-20 minutes and then leave for their own worship and teaching. A variation on this is for them to start separately and then come into the service for the last 10-15 minutes. Either way, and there are pros and cons to each one (which we will discuss later), this is probably the easiest way to start out on this path.

During the time the children are present it is vital that their needs are taken into account. Their presence must be acknowledged and responded to. The preacher must be prepared to talk with them, rather than at them, and be prepared for any response. It really is very easy to ask questions and solicit responses. Ask for prayers of thanks; ask open questions that a congregation can respond to. My experience is to expect responses from all ages, not just the children.

Don't forget to repeat what has been said for the benefit of those in the congregation who have difficulty hearing.

Music for the time the children are present has to be carefully thought about and this topic is covered in some length later in this section.

If the children are in for the first part of the service, then the elements might be: some songs suitable for all ages and maybe one or two aimed solely at the children; a sharing session; some kind of story or illustration and perhaps a prayer as the children prepare to leave. After they have gone then you can have prayers of adoration and confession and then the readings. In general I would avoid them while the children are there. Whilst the Old Testament has much to offer us and should not be ignored, imagine children's image of church if all they hear is readings from it (for it generally comes first) and the prayers of confession.

If the children come in at the end you can share with the congregation what they have been doing; then perhaps have some prayers on issues that they have suggested; a couple of lively songs and the blessing. Of course, in many churches they will also come in to share the Communion. Clearly issues about children and Communion will need to be discussed and agreed before this happens. The timing of when the children come back needs to be discussed and agreed with the Sunday school staff as this can be problematic for them. Children hate leaving uncompleted work behind and arrangements should be made for them to complete it afterwards.

Language, but not necessarily ideas (it is a total fallacy that clever ideas need complicated language), needs to be kept simple and at the level of the children. Not everyone has these skills and on the whole this part of the service should be led by a family friendly preacher. This is not always easy to find and the Methodist plan, particularly, can work against this. The church should, perhaps, negotiate with the Superintendent Minister and the local preachers' meeting to see if it is possible to ensure that preachers who are sympathetic to the aims of a family friendly church are the ones planned.

This does not mean that they, themselves, must have the skills to lead the all-age part of a service, for there may be others in the congregation who can do this. It is possible for the Sunday school staff to lead this initial part of the service themselves, but on the whole I would discourage this practice. It is an extra demand upon them, and their key task is to provide interesting, relevant and fun material for the children during the Sunday school. It strikes me as asking too much to ask them to lead 15-20 minutes of the worship too. Using the preacher, worship leader or minister to do this will hopefully give the children a different perspective on the theme, providing this has been communicated to the preacher or the church has made the decision to use the same material (such as SALT or ROOTS – both these publications provide useful material for each Sunday with children of differing ages and also adults in mind) in church and the Sunday school. Sunday school teachers do not always do this very well, but there may be others in a congregation who may feel that they can do this as part of a rota.

This happens at Burbage and Fleggburgh, where this first part of the service is led by a number of lay people and some local preachers who worship in that church.

ii) All-age service

In this service all ages remain together for the whole Sunday service. Many churches have a pattern where perhaps they have three Sundays in the pattern above and then the fourth is an all-age service. These are very difficult to do well and to keep all ages engaged throughout the service is a monumental task. In the past they have often been done so badly that they are only all-age in the sense that all ages stay away from them.

Much that has been said above about acknowledging and responding to the presence of children if they are present for the first few minutes is also true for the whole of an all-age service. The leader(s) must be able to hold the attention of the children (and teenagers) whilst at the same time meeting the needs of the adults for more depth in the message. Leading all-age worship is extremely difficult and so everything possible must be done to help those involved in co-ordinating and leading it.

I find that it is helpful, as a preacher, to have the children sitting together at the front. I know there is something that is good about families sitting together but it is much harder for the preacher to hold the attention of the children. It is a fact that children are nearly always better behaved for other adults than they are for their own parents, and so separation from their parents helps take away the hissed arguments between parent and child during the service. In addition parents nearly always notice their children's behaviour much more than the rest of a congregation and assume that they are irritating everyone else just as much as they are irritating them. This is rarely true.

Add to this that if children are with parents towards the back they cannot see very much and, as much of what is done in all-age services should be visual, these children are missing out greatly. It is also much easier for a leader to interact with the children, asking questions and hearing responses, if they are close. In my experience children respond better when they are together, sometimes egging one another on to give a response.

Somehow these constraints should be balanced with the need stated in the previous chapter to keep families together. This can be done if you are prepared to use a night-club style of layout, where the congregation sits at tables. This seems to be the one format that seems to allow families to sit together without the squabbles described earlier. I suspect this works as the format forces a greater informality than lines of chairs or pews. I have seen this style used very effectively at large Christian gatherings and have also used it once or twice myself, but in the church hall rather than the church itself.

This also allows for activities to be available on the tables. However, I suspect that most congregations are not yet ready for such changes.

Clearly the decision as to whether children sit with their parents or together with their peers is one for parents to make. Some families will want to be together and that is fine, but it is helpful if the child's need to see and participate in what is happening are taken into account when choosing where to sit.

Other factors can help, such as: placing the seats facing the longest wall so that everyone is nearer the worship leader; or placing the chairs in a semi-circle as this has the same impact; or only placing just enough chairs for the congregation, so that folk cannot hide at the back.

There is a perceived wisdom that all-age services should never be longer than 45 minutes, or else the children get fidgety. I have never found this to be true and nor did I when visiting churches to research this book. Are these the same children who can sit entranced by Saturday morning TV for three and a half hours without uttering a word? The secret is not the overall length (worship should never be such torture for anyone of any age that brevity is an advantage!), but keeping the length of each individual part of the service short and maintaining the pace of delivery.

On the whole no one item should be more than four or five minutes in length. Having a period of worship where songs are coupled to prayers can be helpful here. If there is to be a significant sermon, it should be broken up into several parts. That will also help create a good structure for the message.

Keep the pace going. I learnt this whilst leading a beach mission. Children have plenty of things to do on a beach in addition to the mission and are also free to wander off and do largely whatever they want. I discovered that short breaks between different activities in the mission caused their attention to wane and then they wandered off. Even the few seconds it takes a worship band to wander up from their seats, find the right page in the song book, pick up and tune their instruments and be ready to start is sufficient for the mission to lose half the children, as they wander off for a swim, to build a sandcastle or buy ice-creams. I would recommend working on a beach mission team for anyone who wants to learn how to hold children's attention.

This is why announcers talk over the credits of programmes during children's TV. They know that the children's attention will waver even in the few seconds it takes the credits to whiz up the screen and that they will use the remote control to change channels.

Do not have any periods (however short) of inactivity. Make sure that the service is well planned and that everybody involved knows what they are doing and when they are doing it, so that they are up and ready to go at the appropriate moment.

Silent prayer can be used, but any period of silent prayer should be introduced with clear instructions, so that everyone, including the children, knows what to do with the silence.

The more the preacher presents visually the better and not only for the children's sake. Research has shown that adults, too, absorb much more when it is presented to them visually rather than orally. This can be seen in the business world where virtually no business person would ever think of making a presentation without the support of a set of slides, either on card or acetate or by using data projection. Yet most preachers try to do the same thing without any visual support.

There are many different ways of using visual aids. One of the most common ways is to bring something to show people and to talk about it. On the whole it is best to bring something large that everyone can see, but I have seen preachers get away with something small by either making a joke of it or passing the object around the congregation.

A screen can be used in a host of different ways. Either OHP or data projection can be used very effectively. Photographs, illustrations, puzzles, quizzes, icons, video clips can all be displayed easily. Even if preachers just put the bullet points of their sermon onto the screen it would make a huge difference to how much of the message was absorbed. (See the section on using projectors.)

My experience as I have travelled around is that all-age worship is best delivered with a measured informality and a gentle good humour. It is not a crime to be entertaining and to make a congregation laugh. All the great preachers I have heard have been able to entertain and amuse, just before delivering a knock-out punch.

iii) Multiplexed services

In these services the congregation is split into two. The split may be in the context of time, where two congregations use the same building at different times, perhaps one in the morning and another in the evening, or perhaps two services of different styles on a Sunday morning. The split can also be based on premises, where two congregations meet in two different places at the same time, perhaps one in the church and another in the hall, or perhaps in two different church buildings simultaneously.

In the situation of a church plant it is possible for the split to be in both place and time. This occurs when a new congregation has been planted on neutral territory at a time other than the worship time of the existing congregation. This may be in a village hall, a school etc. The reason for picking a neutral venue in this way is to encourage those who are not used to walking into a church to come in. Regular worshippers often seriously underestimate how difficult it is to make that initial entrance through the church doors.

There are a number of common situations where this multiplexing already happens. There are many churches where the morning and evening services have two very different congregations. There are others where two congregations have been merged to form one church for administration and pastoral oversight, but they still continue to worship in their separate buildings. A very common situation is where the children go every week to a Sunday school in another part of the building.

In many ways these are an admission of failure. The failure is that it is impossible for two congregations to worship as one. The differences may be any combination of style, theology, churchmanship, education or background. The gospel implication is that we should be able to overcome these differences, but many congregations find that they simply cannot accommodate the breadth of styles and ages within their own social make-up.

There is always a danger that the gap between the congregations will broaden. This can be seen in some churches that have a separate Sunday school. The gap widens between the two and the Sunday school runs virtually as a separate agency to the church. This can happen also where two congregations share the same building at different times.

This is a way of accepting that the days when the majority of people worshipped in their local church are over. It is my experience that people, and particularly families, are prepared to travel some distance to attend the church that suits their preferred style of worship and has the facilities to cater for their children. It seems that in society we are so used to being consumers and having a choice that we are also exercising this over where and how we choose to worship.

It appears that multiplexing is a way of allowing people to exercise this choice. There are different ways of making this work.

One way is allowing different churches to develop their own 'house style'. I see this particularly in Anglican churches in urban areas. Each parish church may offer a different style of worship, as here in King's Lynn, where one is Anglo-Catholic, another is middle-of-the-road and the civic church, another is an LEP, and the fourth is informal and evangelical. Their congregations are drawn from around the town and bear very little resemblance to the parish boundaries. In many ways they are offering a multiplexed system based on different buildings in the town.

I think the Methodist Church could learn from this. At the moment local preachers seem to be planned around the churches in such a way that prevents churches from developing their own style and ways of doing things. The plan system when used unimaginatively just plonks preachers of varying styles onto churches and prevents each church from developing a flavour of its own. Although this could be argued as being a desirable system in terms of breadth, my experience is that this is not actually what many congregations want these days. I believe it would be beneficial slowly to change how the plan is created, perhaps working towards a system where churches are encouraged to invite preachers from a list of approved preachers on a plan and then inform the Superintendent whom they have asked. This would give churches the freedom to ask the preachers who could manage the style of worship that the church preferred. It would allow a church to develop a distinctive flavour while still ensuring that the preachers used were fully trained and approved by the Methodist Church. Generally such models are much harder to implement in rural areas, as there is a lesser density of churches and a greater reluctance to travel.

Another way is to establish two congregations in one building, by having two services at different times. This may already be happening if a church has morning and evening services that are of a different style and appeal to different congregations. However, this could also happen on a Sunday morning with coffee served between the services. My experience is that there will be some tensions over the timings and one service will have to be earlier than most people like, and the other later. This means that there will have to be some compromises.

Yet another way is to meet at the same time, but use different space for the two services, perhaps one in the hall and the other in church. There can be a tendency, which must be resisted, for the congregation that meets in the church to see themselves as the 'proper congregation'. Clergy have to work hard at being seen equally in the two congregations regardless of their own preferences. This may mean that they may have to develop new skills.

If congregations are divided in this way it is vital that some ways are engineered for the two congregations to meet and relate to one another in ways other than in the inevitable business meetings. In the churches I have visited which work in this way I have discovered that worshipping together is probably not the right way to do this. At one church when I was present it was announced that the following Sunday service was to be all-age worship with the traditional congregation, and the groans from the children were very telling. At another they had given up worshipping together except on very rare occasions, as significant numbers of both congregations either stayed away or went and worshipped elsewhere.

Another model is to plant a new church in a different building, perhaps a school hall or community centre. This is a model designed to attract people who are not used to coming to church. For some these days, walking in through the front door of a church can be quite a daunting experience. Worshipping in a hall or school can help take away this initial reluctance. It also allows a congregation to be more flexible, perhaps working in a way that might be seen by some as unacceptable in a church, or in a way that a church building simply cannot accommodate.

4

Elements of all-age worship

No matter which combinations of models from the previous chapter are used there will be a number of common elements within those models. These elements make up the worship and teaching. This section seeks to explore how these can best be used in all-age congregations. This means any worship at which more than one generation, including children, may be present.

i) Music

Music is something that can make or break a service. So often it seems that, as a preacher and worship leader, I work very hard to use music to create a shape and a mood in worship to have it wrecked by an organist who plays a hymn or chorus either much too slowly or, less commonly, much too quickly. Such things can spoil a service and so it is important to get the music in our churches right. This is not only true for those churches that are seeking to be family friendly, but for all of our churches. Sadly we must face up to the fact that in many of our churches the music is far from right!

This does not mean that we should all be singing modern hymns but rather we should do what we do well, and that there should be a mix of the old and new. Children must also be catered for.

On the whole children aged less than nine are not able to read fluently enough to sing at the same time, unless they already know the song. So the best types of songs for these are therefore short repetitive ones that can be learnt. They should for the most part be quite lively and one must question whether the organ is the most suitable instrument for them. You may consider using a guitarist or a modern keyboard for the first part of the service. It is a good idea for the Sunday school staff to work out a list of songs that the children know and like and for this to be communicated to those preparing and leading the worship.

There are not a lot of good children's hymns around, so it might be better to include a number of popular lively choruses in this list.

The language of hymns can be a problem for many people these days. I am not talking about 'thee', 'thou' and 'ye' as these can be explained to children in just a few seconds. In fact the whole exercise could be made fun by getting them to talk to each other in such language. I'm talking about heavy theological language or words that have changed their meaning (get children to draw you an 'angel train' and you'll soon see what I mean).

The issue of inclusive language is just as important for children's hymns as those for adults. Perhaps here it is even more important as the right approach will engender good habits from the beginning in children and young people.

Look out also for the theology of children's hymns. We can all understand how the words of the children's hymns of the past have given us wrong understandings of Jesus or of his message; for example, 'Gentle Jesus, meek and mild' or 'You in your small corner and I in mine' now make me cringe. I am sure, though, that some of the modern children's songs will also be looked at in a similar light in years to come.

Many of the case study churches chose not to use children's hymns at all, preferring to pick a mixture of adult worship songs that children could understand. The words of these are modern and clear and others have a repeated chorus which is much better for those who cannot quite read well enough yet. They believe that children can gain much from these. If you are picking songs deliberately for children then be cautious and make sure that the worship content is sufficient to justify their inclusion.

Permit and encourage younger children to join in either with percussive instruments, banners, or streamers (see Dance and movement, page 48).

Project the words if possible. Not only does this help a congregation to sing better by encouraging them to look up, but it also frees the hands for clapping or actions. If a song has actions then encourage everyone to do them. The message communicated to children by those adults who stand there frozen is very negative and unhelpful. Perhaps those adults who feel silly doing such actions should think about Paul's injunction to be 'fools for Christ'.

Use a good mix of hymns. Do not think that only modern hymns are suitable for all-age congregations for we have many fine and lively traditional hymns. The work that my wife and I have done producing the MIDI files on the Family Friendly Churches Web Site has cleared any doubts that I had about this. Most of these hymn tunes are robust, solid and uplifting when played well by a fine musician on a good instrument. The problem is that far too often in worship they are played too slowly and without any feeling, on an awful organ.

Far too many churches have organs that are simply appalling instruments of torture. These are those dreadful home organs from the 60s and 70s, which people no longer wanted to give houseroom, so they donated them to the church. Many have been given away because the family have bought a new one and the only other alternative is the tip (which is where most of them belong). I have a huge number of these scattered around my circuit and they have done immense damage to the quality of worship. Churches even replace them when they are offered another one believing that the new one cannot sound as bad as the old one. They invariably do! Most organs produced before the mid-

1990s sound dreadful and should not be confused in any way with modern digital organs that produce an excellent sound.

A modern £500 keyboard will sound better than most of these 'donated' (I think I prefer the word 'dumped') organs. If you buy a keyboard equipped with a floppy disk drive, it is very easy to use MIDI files. You do not then need a musician at all to provide the accompaniment. In many cases modern clavinovas are proving to be very suitable for use in churches.

Coupled with a worn out and out-of-date instrument, so often, is a poor organist. I know that some of these people have played on valiantly for many years and need to be commended for this, but they really can be a mixed blessing. So many of them say to me: 'Well, I'm not really an organist, I learnt to play the piano.' Some of them even say this to me while sitting at an organ that is placed right next to a piano. Surely even basic common sense should dictate that if you have a pianist, then they should play the piano, and not attempt to play an instrument that is quite different and needs different skills. The irony is that, in many of our churches, the piano is probably a far better quality instrument than the organ it sits next to and added to this, in my experience, small congregations sing better when accompanied by a piano. Organs only really work well when played by a fine organist in a large church. Our smaller churches should stop attempting to be large ones and use what they have to maximum effect.

All churches need to look at their music critically to see if there is a better way of producing it. The sad truth is that for far too long in our churches music has been synonymous with an organist (or pianist) playing an organ. This seriously needs to be broadened. So look around your congregation and ask a number of questions. What musicians do we have? What instruments do they play? Are they willing to play for worship? If they are playing already, are they playing the right instrument? Is there any way we can create a group of musicians to play together?

The trouble is that far too many people have got so used to our great hymns being played too slowly on a dreadful instrument that they now believe that they like it that way. We all need to have our expectations lifted.

ii) Reading of Scripture

Somehow we have to make the experience of reading from the Bible a positive one for children, as surely it is our hope that they will acquire the good habit of reading Scripture on their own account. Choice of passages, translations and readers are vital in all of this.

When dealing with Scripture make sure that the choice of passage is appropriate. Clearly long lists of begetting or lists of laws, or complex Pauline theology may not be right in this environment. In fact, just reading these straight in churches probably doesn't suit adults either. It is much better to try to unravel Paul in a Bible study group. Keep the passages relatively short and relevant to the message that is being given. Do not be afraid to trim long passages given in the lectionary.

The translation is critical. It is much better to use modern, clear translations that are easily understood by children and adults. The King James Version should not be used. The language is outdated, not just because of 'thee' and 'thou', but because some other words like 'charity' and 'fear' have changed their meaning since this translation was made. As someone who has studied the development of Greek New Testaments since printing began for part of a doctorate, I probably understand more than most the inherent weaknesses of the Greek manuscripts that lay behind the King James Version.

Modern translations (with the exception of the New King James Version) are based on Greek manuscripts that are much more likely to be close to what Matthew, Mark, Luke, John and Paul actually wrote. Please do use them. It is best for a church to decide which translation it will use and then supply that translation as pew Bibles. If looking afresh for Bibles then a church should consider an inclusive modern language version in straightforward English.

Having Bibles in the pews is helpful to teach children to follow the reading in a Bible, but not only children. I, and no doubt many other adults, find it immensely helpful to follow the text of a Bible reading as it is read aloud. Nothing is more irritating than to pick up a Bible from the pew, find the passage and then discover that the preacher has decided to read from a different translation. Please discourage preachers from doing this. If a theological point depends on a particular translation, then take my word for it, it is probably a weak one.

It is helpful if the reference of the reading is announced twice and supplemented by the page number in the pew Bibles. In doing this it should be noted that the pagination of a lectern Bible is not always that of the smaller pew edition.

Finally, select readers carefully. The overriding necessity is that a reader must be heard and also have a strong voice. Even the best microphones cannot compensate for a reader who mumbles or gabbles. Readers must be trained and prepared to use a microphone if the church has a sound system with a loop. A good reader will be able to vary pitch, tone, pace and colour of sound to make the reading more interesting.

If you ask children to read, which on the whole is a good idea, note that they are quite capable of reading the passage over and over again quite perfectly in rehearsal and then mumbling and gabbling their way through it when faced with a live congregation. Some patience and understanding will be needed. Do pick your best readers, as the prime objective is that the meaning of the passage is communicated to the congregation. If you are unsure then it is a good idea to ensure that the text is available to the congregation in some other form.

In all-age services consider using any of the following tips:

Dramatised readings using several voices make readings more interesting and easier to understand. You do not need to buy expensive versions to do this (see Drama, page 44).

The Psalms are often used in a responsive way. This works well because most of the Psalms were written as Hebrew poetry in which each idea is stated in two different ways. This means they are ideal for responsive reading. The standard way is for the leader to read the first part of the stanza (usually in light text) and then the congregation to respond with the restatement of the idea in the second part of the stanza (usually in bold text). This can, of course, be varied; you can split the congregation into two parts, left side/right side, front/back, male/female, adults/children.

It is effective sometimes, instead of simply reading a passage, to tell it as a story in your own words. To add interest tell the story from the viewpoint of a minor character or even tell it in the first person as if you were that character. Consider using drama or mime to put over a reading.

If you have projection available then project the words of the reading onto the screen as it is read. Do ensure that you are using exactly the same version. Another good idea is to project images that support the story as it is told. Either these can be produced by an artist in the congregation, scanned from an illustrated Bible, taken from clipart books or CD-ROMs or downloaded from the internet.

If you have video projection available then consider using a clip from a 'Jesus' film instead of a reading. Do check out the films carefully first. I once made the mistake of showing to a group of teenagers Joan Collins, as Potiphar's wife, eating Donny Osmond alive in the film version of *Joseph and the Amazing Technicolor Dreamcoat*.

The biblical software, iLumina[1] has a number of animated readings available. These read the text from the Bible and animate the story at the same time. The sections on the building of the tabernacle are particularly helpful in showing how the tabernacle and different artefacts might have looked and were constructed. If you have data projection then these can be projected onto a main screen.

Do remember when considering these options that the presentation of the biblical text comes first and is the overriding consideration. Do not allow the presentation to subdue the truth of the passage, but since we live in a visual age, do search out creative ways of using images to draw out the truth of the passage.

iii) Prayers

Prayer is an important part of any service. Prayer is an enormous privilege; when we pray we are talking to the God who created a universe greater than we can imagine and we believe and experience that we are heard. Everything we do in prayers during worship should try to communicate the importance of prayer and foster habits of personal prayer in our children.

A general rule ought to be that the language should be simple but not simplistic. The most wonderful and complex ideas can be put over in simple language. Avoid complicated and jargon-riddled 'prayer language' at all costs and please avoid repeating the words 'just' and 'Lord'.

One way of helping to draw the congregation in is to ask them for ideas for prayers. This is particularly helpful for prayers of thanksgiving, intercession and petition. I remember leading a fun day on a particularly deprived estate. The children had been very difficult and unco-operative all afternoon and then we came to a prayer time. I asked them if they had anything to pray for and they all came up with the name of a local teenager who had recently been killed while 'joy-riding'. Just for those five minutes the mood changed and they stood in silence as I led the prayers. The importance of prayers had been communicated simply by asking what they wanted to pray about and verbalising their feelings to the God who made this world. As in all instances when a response is requested, adults should also be invited to respond.

In school assemblies I have always found the 'prayer drill' useful for bringing children into prayer. I first came across this being done effectively in the all-age worship at a large Christian gathering. All the children – and some of the staff – rotate their right hands in the air, then their left hands, followed by a barrel roll concluded with a single clap of the hands as they are brought together in prayer. Stress that after the clap there must be absolute silence as we are talking to God and that is important. I have found that, on the whole, even the teachers like this.

Projected illustrations and photographs can be used as an aid to prayer, perhaps to help us to focus on our prayers of thanksgiving, or to focus our intercessions. Ready sources of photographs are available from the internet and there are a number of 'news' sites that may be a good source for pictures. Perhaps even some video clips from the news itself could be used in a powerful way. These would have to be very much up to date and would probably be best presented without sound. It is important to note that, although it is easy to download and use such images in worship, you may well be breaking the copyright of the originators of the material when you use it in this way. It is best to check and seek permission to use the material in the way you want. My experience has been that information providers are generally willing to give permission when I have explained the purpose for which I want to use the material.

In using visual aids it is important to stress to congregations that it is perfectly valid to pray with our eyes open and looking up.

It might be possible to couple the images with some music or just use music on its own. This needs to enhance prayer rather than overwhelm it, and so whatever is used should be kept at a reasonably quiet level, though not so quiet that it cannot be heard. If you are using a data projector then the music can be generated by the PC as PowerPoint™ displays the pictures, though the sound will need to be amplified in some way. See 'Projection' in the chapter 'Using technology in worship'.

It is vitally important that children should be encouraged to pray for themselves and also to pray out loud. This can best be done by giving everyone clear guidelines and making it clear that no special 'prayer language' is required. For instance, it would be possible in prayers of thanksgiving to get children (and adults) to shout out their prayers in the form of 'Thank you, God, for ...'. If used for intercessions then this could be, for instance, coupled with coming out to the front and lighting a candle, perhaps with the words 'I light this candle for ...'.

The worst discouragement for non-confident pray-ers, both adults and children, are those who seem able to pray aloud in complex, old-fashioned language for a long period of time. Find gentle ways of discouraging this at all costs. It may make it easier for beginners if the congregation is divided into small groups to pray together. Whenever dividing an all-age congregation into groups try to find ways of mixing the ages in the different groups. It is helpful to give clear instructions to the groups and to back these up on a screen if you have one. Do also remember that people whose hearing is not 100 per cent (like me) have trouble differentiating their group's voices from the general background hubbub.

Do not be afraid to ask children to write prayers and read them as part of a prayer time. They can sometimes come up with prayers that are quite special. Another way of writing prayers is to distribute paper in some form, for example, green paper as leaves on a tree. Invite people to write prayers on them and come to the front and pin them onto a central display.

A service conducted recently at London Rd Methodist Church in King's Lynn had a number of prayer displays spread around the room, giving information about certain issues. Some of the displays had scrolling PowerPoint™ presentations on laptops but this is not essential. People were invited to wander from display to display to make their prayers.

The congregational response during prayers is a good way of drawing people into prayers.

In Cromer the '10 to 10' service has a prayer notice-board on which issues are pinned. The whole board is brought to the front and the prayers are drawn from the board. Wiveton parish church has a children's prayer book which is kept in the children's chapel at the back of the church. These prayers were read during the all-age service by the older children.

It is useful to invite people to make some kind of action to symbolise the prayers that they are offering. This could be the lighting of candles, pebbles placed in a bowl of water, sticking prayers onto a board or many other kinds of response.

iv) Communion

How much participation children should have in Communion is a big question. The key question is whether or not children should take the bread and wine. There are seemingly four groups that should have a say as to whether Communion is given to a child or not.

1) The first view is that of the children. Their views should count and children and young people hold a whole range of opinions. Some want to take the bread and wine at an early age, others (especially teenagers) have made a decision to wait until Confirmation. A child may opt to take Communion when very young and then decide not to as they reach their teenage years. Involving the children in the process of deciding or not whether they take Communion is also a good way of demonstrating that this is an important decision to make and that Communion should not be taken lightly.

The best way is probably to get them to talk about Communion with their own leaders – dragging them into a church council will only faze them. As it is likely that you will want to prepare them for Communion (and reinforce that prep-aration from time to time) then that discussion could be linked to teaching and preparation.

2) Secondly there are the parents. Parents vary as to whether they wish their children to receive the elements or not. When families take Communion together then this is very easy. When I am distributing, if a child I don't know raises their hands for Communion then I glance quickly at the parent to seek their permission.

This is not so easy when the parents of a child are not in church themselves. I suspect it would be wise for a letter to go out to parents seeking the permission to give their children Communion. You need to be clear as to whether you are operating an 'opt in' or 'opt out' system and what the church will do if no response is received from the parent.

3) The third group are ministers. Ministers have definite views as to whether they personally should give the elements to children. Clearly if the minister of the church is totally against it then this should be respected and corrected at the next invitation if it is different to the desired policy of the church. Care should be taken with visiting ministers and they should have the church's policy made clear to them. On the whole life is much easier if a church sticks to using ministers who are in broad agreement with the church's policy on Communion and children.

4) Lastly is the policy of the church. The giving of Communion to children is an issue that should be discussed and decided at church council. Like so many issues in a council meeting, it is best if a consensus is arrived at, rather than having a vote with the inevitable winners and losers.

However, there are a number of arguments against giving Communion to children that may need to be countered as the issue is discussed.

'They don't understand it.' This is the most common argument applied against giving Communion to children. It is true that children do not understand Communion, but then neither do adults. No one fully understands what is happening as we share bread and wine in this way. It is a mystery operating at several levels. So if the requirement is to 'understand Communion' then no one, not even the adults, could take it. The only requirement, surely, is that children are taught that it is important and they should be encouraged to take it seriously. This can be done in Sunday school in the build-up to an occasion when children will be invited to take Communion.

'They are not yet confirmed.' Most Methodist churches operate an open table, usually inviting adults to share Communion whether they are members of any church or not. This policy can be traced back to John Wesley's conviction that Communion was a 'converting' sacrament as well as a 'confirming' one. It seems odd that we are willing to give Communion to adults who have just walked in off the street but not to the children and young people who are with us every week. It is interesting to note how other denominations deal with this. Roman Catholic children take their first Communion at the age of around seven or eight and usually several years before Confirmation. While some Anglican churches insist that children wait until Confirmation, an increasing number now invite children to share fully in Communion.

Whether or not we should give Communion to children who are not yet baptised poses a real issue. Many committed church families now do not have their children baptised, rather opting for a thanksgiving service. This service is chosen in the hope that the children will make a commitment to Jesus followed by adult baptism probably by total immersion, when they have themselves come to faith. I have never known a non-church family opt for this. If we insist upon baptism as a qualification for receiving Communion we could end up in the ludicrous position of including children of families who have little or no contact with the church, and excluding those whose families are the most committed.

Most church leaders I have spoken to about this issue have confirmed that, in the right circumstances, they would be willing to give the elements to a child who had not yet been baptised.

When a church has discussed the issue at church council then there are a number of models that can be applied.

1) Always send the children out to Sunday school during Communion. This is simply a way of avoiding the issue. If this model is applied then it is a shame that a significant part of the church family is never present for this very important part of the church's life together. Remember that this strategy excludes not only the children, but also their leaders, who may find it difficult to take Communion at other times.

2) Bring the children back in for Communion. Some churches start that service separately and then the children are brought back in for Communion. There are two points in the service when this can best be done. The Offertory/Peace just

before the Prayer of Thanksgiving is one, and just as the Communion is being served is another. At both these times there is a reasonable amount of movement and the arrival of children will not be too disruptive. My own belief is that if children are to take Communion then they should be present for the Prayer of Thanksgiving which, in its own way, explains and sets the scene for what is to follow. If you use this model then please note that, in my experience, it is not popular with Sunday school leaders who have to finish their work quickly at what is inevitably a variable time.

3) Have an all-age Communion service once in a while, say, once a quarter. Here the children stay in for a whole Communion service which is itself designed to be family friendly using the principles outlined in this book. There is an illustrated service book, *At the Breaking of the Bread,*[2] available for this purpose, which is now also available as a set of PowerPoint™ slides to supplement the book. There is also a sample of the PowerPoint™ version of the Christmas Communion services on the CD-ROM that accompanies this book.

4) Hold all-age Communion services at a different time to the main service. This may seem an odd idea, but I have seen it done very successfully in a small village church. The whole congregation met once a month for an all-age Communion service before the main service. The Communion was open to the whole church, including children. They then shared a hearty breakfast before moving back into church for the main morning service.

These models can be used even if you are not content to give Communion to children. In these circumstances children should be invited to the rail to receive a blessing. In all instances clear instructions should be given as to how to receive Communion and how to indicate that one would like a blessing instead. The surest way is to ask people who do not wish to receive to keep their hands firmly by their side or bring their service sheet with them. Whatever system is adopted it should be clearly understood by everyone including those distributing Communion. Some system may also need to be adopted to help those of any age who have a gluten-free diet and therefore require gluten-free bread.

v) Drama

Drama is a very powerful medium for putting a message across. Plays, films and TV can make us laugh, cry, horrify us and challenge us – sometimes at the same time. Churches can use drama to prompt the same emotions and also to grab the attention.

In fact the whole act of worship is a drama from beginning to end. I remember taking my two small children to a very high Anglican mass several years ago. We were worried about their behaviour during this, particularly if they became bored. We needn't have worried, as they sat absolutely transfixed as they watched the drama of the mass unfold before them. There was almost constant movement between the priest, servers and choir as they paraded, carried the gospel book, used incense and went through the

Communion. All this was a drama that held them spellbound.

In our worship we need to use the techniques of drama to make it interesting. Different speakers, movement and changes of mood, colour and tone can all help in this. Each speaker needs to develop good habits of changing the volume, pitch and speed of their voice. There is nothing worse than the preacher/worship leader who conducts the whole act of worship him/herself, delivered in a monotone, head down, reading from notes. The section on 'The Sermon' will look at how this can be avoided.

Within the drama of worship itself we can use different types of drama to get the message across in an interesting way.

The first way, and we do this in most churches, is the congregational response. We are so used to this that it happens automatically. For instance, if I say, 'Lord, in your mercy', most congregations will respond 'hear our prayer'. There are many examples of this. There are a number of prayers that we all say together; most notably the Lord's Prayer. The effect of all of this is to draw a congregation into the drama of the whole worship.

Getting the congregation to respond during a talk is a way of drawing them back into that presentation. For example, at each change of point in your structure, get them to report back what the previous points were. Or you might at some point ask them a question, perhaps turning an illustration into a question (as described above) or asking them how they feel about something. All this helps to maintain their interest in what is happening. Worship should not be a lecture, it should be a shared activity involving both leader and people, and the more we encourage that sharing the more interesting worship can be. There really is no reason on earth why worship should be dull and boring – that is not what God intended for us!

A very easy way of making a reading more interesting is to use a dramatised reading, where several voices are used. For example, one person could function as the narrator, a second person reading Jesus's words, and a third voice reading the words of whoever Jesus is talking to. This instantly gives variation, depth and interest to the reading providing you use readers who can put this expression into the text.

The Dramatised Bible[3] has a major part of the Bible presented as dramatised readings, but it is quite expensive. If you have a CCLI licence then you are permitted to photocopy it so that each reader can have a copy of the words. However, I have to say that it is a very thick book and I have always found it difficult to photocopy well.

If you have a PC and a copy of the Bible on it then there really is an easy way of producing dramatised readings. Find the passage that you want and highlight it. Then use 'Edit' and 'Copy' or Ctrl + C to copy it into the clipboard, switch to your word processing software and use 'Edit' and 'Paste' to paste it into a blank document. It is then an easy matter to break this passage into different voices. In 'Word for Windows' it can be made to look like a script using 'Format' and 'Paragraph' and then an indent with a hanging first line. Then simply print out the number of copies required.

As an aside not all computerised versions of the Bible allow you to copy the text into the clipboard. As this is a very useful function then you should ask the salesperson about it before you purchase. If you have access to the internet then there are a number of web sites that have the text of the Bible on them, all of which can be used in this way. http://www.biblegateway.com/cgi-bin/bible offers several translations, though most of them are non-inclusive and, for copyright reasons, rather out of date.

Another option is to use instant drama and this can be great fun. As you tell a story get some volunteers to mime the actions, for example, using people as the two houses, one on sand, the other on rock, or as Jesse's sons coming before Samuel, or as David and Goliath. The possibilities are endless. I have found that most children (and many adults) are willing to volunteer for this and readily throw themselves into the drama – so be prepared to be upstaged! My experience has been that this technique works very well with primary school children.

Don't read the story from the Bible as that would just kill the whole thing. Tell the story from memory and, as the story progresses, you should be prepared to be in the middle of your cast and give stage directions as the action unfolds.

This can be coupled with mass congregation participation if there is a crowd to portray. For instance, imagine the two armies in David and Goliath glaring at each other across the aisle. Think of the crowd which is amazed by what Jesus does, or shouting 'Hosanna' on Palm Sunday, or even 'Crucify him' later in the week.

For the last few years SALT has produced an instant drama for an all-age service over Christmas. Many of these have been great fun. I have found that children have thrown themselves into these instant nativity plays with great gusto. They don't need costumes or props, they can be improvised, and most certainly don't need rehearsal after rehearsal, because children know the story and instinctively know how to portray it in a drama.

All the above are great fun; they help to get a story or point across and require no rehearsal. However, if you do have a group that is prepared to meet and practise then the scope widens even more.

The easiest style of drama to produce is the narrator(s) and mime version. One or more narrators read their lines and the cast act out the drama. These are easy to prepare because there is no learning of lines and so one can be prepared (or even written) over an evening and be ready for worship the following Sunday. Using more than one narrator is helpful as it gives a change of voice and there are a number of extra possibilities of humour in the interaction of the narrators. These could, perhaps, be characters themselves commenting on what is happening, for example, God and Satan in the story of Job.

Even though this is a simple and quick way of producing drama, do make sure that adequate time is given to rehearsal so that everyone has clear and big actions to perform, and knows exactly what they have to do and when. Every effort should be made to ensure that it is well produced.

If there is a really important line that needs to be emphasised, then let the characters in the drama say that line for themselves. This will have a great impact on the congregation and it isn't hard to learn just one line.

In most books of drama there are usually a number of sketches of this type.

The next step is what I call 'Generation Game' drama. The cast have the script in front of them, either obviously, or hidden in different props. For a holiday club we once did a series of sketches where the words were projected onto the wall behind the audience of children, using an OHP. This cuts down on the learning time, but the piece must still be well rehearsed so that the scripts act as a prompt, rather than just being read.

These techniques are acceptable when time is pressured, but generally it is very difficult to perform and read your lines at the same time. I suspect that, on the whole, it is better to do fewer dramas and take the time to learn lines and practise fully.

There is an exception to this and it is the use of puppets. Using glove puppets the real performers are hidden behind a screen and so can easily get away with having a script pinned up for reading.

However, even here there must be enough practice to ensure that the script is acting as a prompt, rather than just being read.

It might be thought that puppets are just for children, but there are today a number of groups around which use puppets to put a message across to all ages. In the right hands puppets can be used to express all the sensitivity and emotions of live actors.

At one of the churches I visited extensive but informal use was made of puppets. The young man introducing the theme used one and had largely taught himself not to move his lips as he spoke for it (though he did avoid Ms and Bs). This proved to be very effective. Only very accomplished performers like Steve Wild can get away with moving their lips. Another way of using puppets in this informal way is to have the puppet whisper his/her responses directly into the ear.

To present a drama fully in worship can be extremely effective but takes a considerable amount of effort. Time spent learning lines and rehearsing will always pay dividends when presenting drama. For this to work well you need a committed drama group who will meet weekly to develop and rehearse drama. Even then it is probably asking too much to ask them to do more than an item a month. However, such a drama group is a good way of drawing young people into the life of the church. There is a huge amount of material around for such groups.

For a really special occasion it is possible to hire the services of a professional Christian theatre company.

These are not cheap and you will have to be sure that your church will underwrite, so that you are not left to fill the gap between the cost of the company and the receipts at the door. I have often found it difficult to break even with such events, but the underwriting could be seen as a way of funding mission. It is vital that you spend time with the company pinning down exactly what you want them to do and how this can fit in with your overall strategy for the church. Time spent on publicising such events is usually time well spent.

If you have a LCD projector or a very large TV screen then it is possible to show video clips as part of a service. This can be done either by connecting a DVD or video player to the projector, or by scanning video into your PC (you may need special hardware – and a huge hard disk) and then inserting it into PowerPoint™ in order to display it. In either case you will need to amplify the sound. See the section on Projection for more details.

Do check out any copyright issues, but I have found companies to be helpful in this. I once wanted to use a clip from *Who wants to a Millionaire?* and modify it for my own purposes. I contacted the makers, Celador, and found them most helpful.

There are a number of good films about the life of Jesus that can be used. Care needs to be taken, however, as directors can interpret the biblical text in their own way. Worthy of mention is *The Miraclemaker*, which is quite faithful to the biblical text, and comes with permission to show small clips.

There are now a number of Bible programs available that incorporate video clips. Generally your licence to use the software includes using the clips outside the program. This means that with a little rooting around you should be able to find the video files (usually *.AVI) and build them into a PowerPoint™ presentation to use as part of worship.

Worthy of note is iLumina[4] (www.ilumina.com), which has a number of animated video clips and an amazing 'virtual tour' of Jerusalem alongside the biblical text, an encyclopaedia and a library of photographs. Much of this could be used creatively in worship. No doubt other similar products will emerge in the future.

vi) Dance and movement

I love watching dance and I adore the ballet. Dance appeals directly to my emotions in ways that the spoken word and music alone cannot match. The movement and expression of a fine ballerina can express feelings that for many cannot be communicated in any other way. Always in faith we are struggling to express the inexpressible in mere words and yet dance, at its very best, can communicate faith and mystery for many people at a level beyond any other medium. In the light of all this it is laughable to suggest, as has been the case in the past, that dance and movement play no part in worship. As far as we can tell, they were very much part of the worship that Jesus would have known.

Unfortunately I have been gifted with two left feet and no sense of rhythm and so am forced to leave the expression of this art to others. The problem with dance is that when it is done well it is moving beyond words, but when done badly it is comical beyond belief. The secret is always to take steps to ensure that when it is done, it is done well. I think here the responsibility lies with the worship leader to view any offering and try to find tactful ways of suggesting that a piece may not yet be ready for worship.

Ensure firstly that the music is appropriate for worship and can be heard by both the dancers and congregation. Ensure that the piece has been adequately thought through and practised. There is a tendency to go for a 'Laura Ashley' floaty style of dance and this is fine when done well, but it should be noted that this is not the only way dance can be done.

My experience with young people has shown me that many teenage girls (usually 13 to around 15) love to express themselves in dance. They are quite capable of working together to choreograph a piece and bring it as an offering in worship and so this should be encouraged. If there is an adult who is able and willing to help and advise them then this should also be encouraged. But be prepared, most of them will want to move on from this stage.

There is no reason why, with some inventiveness and creativity, disabled people cannot take part in such activities. However, I have only once persuaded boys to take part, but sense that over time this may change.

When using dancers please ensure that the rooms are kept warm, both for rehearsals and performances. This is to minimise the injuries that can be caused by exercising with cold muscles.

All that has been said here about dance can also be applied to mime. Again, this is a way of presenting stories and situations from the Bible that can draw out the underlying emotions. Some of the most effective presentations I have seen in worship have been those of a professional mime artist.

Of course, all of these options require individuals or a team of people with a talent and preparedness to use that talent in worship. This is not always the case for every church, but it would not be right to think that all dance and movement has to be done by a special group at the front of the church. There are a number of other ways that dance and movement can be brought into worship.

The most common way is to use songs with actions. Children love these songs and some adults appreciate the opportunity to stretch out a little. It is best if the words of such songs are either projected or learnt as it is very difficult to do the actions whilst holding a hymn book. If actions are being used then it is vital that as many as possible of the adult congregation do join in. Unfortunately, if even a small number of adults stand there with their arms folded in a determined attempt not to join in the children will quickly get the message that this is 'kids' stuff' and then become very inhibited. This will destroy what can be a very enjoyable experience for children and some adult members of the congregation. If someone needs both hands to hold onto their walking frame then they probably have an excuse not to join in, but otherwise they should be encouraged to take part as enthusiastically as they can.

If you have someone in your congregation who knows sign language then ask them to teach the signs for a song. Anyone who has watched sign language during hymns cannot help but be touched by how expressive it can be. I have found that children in particular pick this up very quickly and remember it easily from one week to the next. I have a group in a village who learnt the signs for a song a couple of years ago, but still remember them with great accuracy. Doing this will affirm anyone in the congregation who is hard of hearing and uses sign language for communication, and it may also encourage one or two hearing people to take the opportunity to learn this most valuable of skills.

For more lively songs it is possible to distribute banners and streamers for children and some adults to use during the song. The colours of the banners have specific meanings and it might be worth exploring these to use as part of an all-age service.

I often couple this with a parade. This goes down well with the children who quite happily follow me around the church. It is best done with a song that is well known as it is difficult to wave a banner, march and read words at the same time. It may be a good idea to make this song the one just before the children leave for their own teaching, then at the end they can parade straight out of the church into their own session. I can remember as a child, on special Sundays in an Anglo-Catholic church, processing around the church as we sang a hymn and, although this was much more formal than I am proposing here, it does show that there is a precedent for such parades.

I have also used movement as part of an address with teenagers and children. Questions are asked and the congregation told: 'If you believe this then stand over here, or this then stand here, and if you think somewhere in between then stand somewhere in between.' When breaking into buzz groups, encourage movement so that the groups are as multi-age as possible.

When I started leading youth services in one church all the teenagers sat in the back two rows. We dealt with this by having a quiz. Whenever they got an answer right they were permitted to move one row forward. By the end of the quiz they were sitting in the front two rows and ready to participate.

I believe that the message has to go out loud and clear that no longer is it necessary to come to church and be compelled to sit still for an hour. Worship today is very much about participation and joining in at all levels, and that includes movement. I have a simple strategy for dealing with congregations with a large number of two to four year olds who will not sit still for an hour, whatever the parents do. It is to introduce so much other movement into the worship that no one notices that these small children are wandering around.

vii) The sermon

The sermon is the most difficult area of all when children are present. The preacher has to present information that will encourage and challenge the adults at their level; (but not teach, for sermons should generally not be used for teaching; teaching should be done in small interactive groups) and at the same time hold the attention of children and young people. It is hard but it can be done.

Firstly, remember that the four- or five-minute rule applies as much to the sermon as the other parts of the service. This does not mean that the preacher should be limited to this, but rather that he or she should break the material down into four- or five- minute bites. The easiest way of doing this is to place a hymn, drama, game or video in between the pieces. For children something active would be best, so avoid using something like a reading to do this.

One of the easiest ways of breaking up the sermon in a way that will draw the children back in is to ask them a question and take responses, though be ready for anything.

Breaking up a sermon into small bites is a good technique as it encourages the preacher to create a good structure for the talk. I don't listen to a lot of sermons, as a minister and paid to give them, but one thing I would be most critical of is the lack of structure in the vast majority of sermons that I have heard. In so many sermons the theology is excellent, the message is well thought out and profound, but because there is no structure it is hard to digest and impossible to remember. Preachers, if you want a congregation to remember what you have said then give your sermon a solid and obvious structure.

One of the best sermons I have ever heard was by Lord Runcie when he was the Archbishop of Canterbury. There is an old adage, 'Tell them what you going to say, tell them, and then tell them what you have said.' This is exactly what he did. For the introduction he outlined the frame-work of what he was going to say. Then he made each point. Each time he changed from one point to the next he reminded us of the points he had made. At the end he then reminded us of each of the points he had made. It was a fine example of how to structure and deliver a sermon.

A good structure and good use of relevant illustrations are important when preaching to any congregation, but become vital when preaching to all-age cong-regations.

I suspect many preachers do not do this because, to them, announcing the structure in this manner feels forced, contrived and repetitive. It only feels like this to preachers because they are the only one who knows the contents of the sermon. To everybody else it is an essential help to allow them to position themselves in the sermon and then to remember it. Only if a sermon has a good and transparent shape will a congregation remember it. The structure does not have to be an introduction, three points and a conclusion. It can be constructed in any reasonable way, but in my opinion an introduction, three points and a conclusion continues to be a good way of putting a sermon together.

The sermon can be even more memorable if there is some element of shape to the structure. For instance, if each point starts with the same letter of the alphabet, for example, the three Cs of marriage (Celebration, Communication and Commitment), or if the points spell out a word, or form the name of a disciple, or the three colours of a candy stick, or anything that sticks in the mind. All this gives the congregation a coat-hanger on which to hang the sermon and consequently to remember it. These things are so important that it is sad that so few preachers seem willing to do this.

There are a number of spin-offs from a good sermon structure.

The first, and where we started this section, is that with a good, clear and transparent shape it is much easier to divide up a sermon into digestible parts. In fact, I would ask any preacher who cannot break a sermon into parts seriously to consider whether to give it all – even to a congregation of adults – in one chunk, for without that underlying framework it will not be memorable.

Secondly, a sermon is much easier to preach without notes if it has a good structure. In fact, preaching without notes generally forces a preacher to prepare a well-organised sermon. In this situation the need of the preacher to remember the sermon for themselves assists the congregation to remember it.

When I was training to be a minister and on placement, the Anglican vicar whose pulpit I was taking over said to me, 'If you want to preach in my church then you do so without notes.' When I protested he said, 'How can you expect a congregation to remember what you have said if you can't?'

I did preach that Sunday without notes and I have hardly ever preached with notes again (only once or twice when I have preached on a very sensitive issue where I have needed to be precise in my wording and able to defend what I have said later!). I do keep notes in my back pocket in case I dry up. I think I have had to refer to them twice in ten years when I have simply forgotten the next point.

Preaching without notes has a number of advantages. Firstly it ensures that your talk has a good framework, because that structure is the means by which you remember. It is not necessary to remember every word, but rather the turning points.

It also means that you can focus on non-verbal communication. There is nothing worse than a preacher who reads a sermon, head down, looking at a full script and having no eye contact with a congregation. Generally this all means that there is often little variation in the tone, pitch, colour of the voice, which will make any preacher sound dull. Adults, let alone children, will switch off quite quickly in this situation.

When preachers use no notes, or minimal notes, they are freed from the lectern or pulpit. Their head is up and there is real eye-to-eye contact. Real communication can now take place. Preachers can see the reactions to what they are saying and if people are looking absorbed then they can expand that point. If they are distracted (and the children fidgeting) they know to accelerate that particular point.

It also means that preachers are free to move and free to use the unspoken details that body language can add to a sermon. Where you stand, how you stand, what you do with your eyes, head and hands are so important. Preaching a sermon is about two-way communication and that can only happen when preachers play their part in it.

Thirdly, with a clear structure it is very easy to produce visual material. It is now accepted that we absorb and remember what we see much better than what we hear. This means that if preachers really want their message to be heard and remembered it should be backed up with visual aids. Even if a preacher were just to use an OHP slide uncovering each point as it was made, the congregation would be greatly assisted in remembering what was said.

Jesus had a wonderful way of using visual aids without even having anything visual to draw upon. He used examples that people were so familiar with that they could simply use their imagination. 'There was a sower ...'; the sight of a sower was an everyday occurrence in that part of the world, and perhaps there was a sower in the next field as Jesus spoke, but the picture is instantly there. 'A woman lost one of her coins ...'; we've all lost things and so this instantly conjures up a picture in our minds of this poor woman frantically searching around her house. Jesus drew so much from the ordinary life of those around that everyone, including children, could picture what he was talking about. It is a skill that all preachers would do well to emulate.

For example, we could talk about someone learning to swim and compare it to growing in faith in Jesus. This is an experience that most of us have gone through, is of direct relevance to children, and so the image is easily conjured up. The preacher could talk of the pool, the water, getting changed, the instructor, being supported and so on.

When children are present we can take this one stage further and turn the whole thing from a story to a discussion. Talking with children will constantly draw them back into what is happening. Try a series of questions: 'Who here can swim?'; 'Where did you learn?'; 'How did you learn?'; 'Did someone hold you in the water?'; 'Did you learn to trust the water?' As always when talking with children be ready for the unexpected response, accept and reflect and then move on, but be careful never to belittle a child and try very hard not to laugh at a comical response. Such a response can put off a child from ever making a response again.

By using this technique you can turn almost any illustration into a discussion and use it to draw children (and adults) back into what is happening. This is one of the key secrets in the leading of all-age worship.

The play and film *Son of Man*, by Dennis Potter, shows Jesus doing just this. Potter's Jesus doesn't just stand up and preach at people. He interacts, draws a response, laughs with them and then makes his point. I am sure this is much closer to the way Jesus delivered his message.

However, I suspect that, in time, we need to move away from a lecture style of preaching to a more participatory style for adults. We all have insights about God and the journey and it is good to share these. One way of doing this is to break into buzz groups for a short period during a sermon. This can work well if a few guidelines are observed. Make sure that the groups know exactly what they have to do. If you have projection available then reinforce the questions by placing them on the screen. Do all you can to mix the generations in the different groups so that insights across the ages can be shared. One of the most successful discussions I have been involved with was when the different ages shared with one another on the issue of sexuality. There was a good deal of sharing and listening and a number of adults commented afterwards how their attitudes and perceptions had been challenged.

One of the churches I visited, 'Escape' at Elburton, ran an all-age Sunday school. 'Escape' is a multiplexed service run in the hall at the same time as the main service in the church. At 'Escape' there was no sermon or address, but rather when the children went out for their separate teaching the adults, too, formed a group and received their teaching and encouragement in this way. This functioned more as a house group and was a time for sharing as well as receiving. It lasted for around 20-25 minutes until the children returned for the closing worship, sharing time and prayers. Despite shorter in time than most Sunday schools this pattern worked well in this environment and is a model that other churches could consider. Finding the right leaders for this is vital to its success, but it is something that could be offered as an option in many churches if there is a space for such a group.

viii) Conclusion

There is a danger that in encouraging participation and creativity in worship the whole service can become a multi-item talent show. This can only be prevented by the preacher ensuring that he or she fully understands why each item is present and how that relates to the overall theme. Time should be spent on giving the service an overall shape, for the point at which each item occurs is also an important consideration.

If an offering is made that is unsuitable, does not fit the theme or simply is not of sufficient quality to lay before God and a congregation (and that's not an easy decision) then the preacher should gently avoid using it in worship.

5

Using technology in worship

Technology makes a good servant, but a very bad master. This should always be borne in mind when using modern technology in churches. When used well it can greatly enhance the worship experience. When used badly and inappropriately it can become distracting and no more than a gimmick.

In most cases this can be avoided by spending time and energy learning how to use it effectively. The people who operate equipment must be sufficiently skilled to make it work, each time, every time. This may well involve going on courses, reading manuals and a lot of practice.

One of the biggest failings is setting up equipment at the last moment. If there is a technical hitch then there is no time either to put it right or to find alternatives. Added to this is the distraction that setting up causes to people who are preparing to worship. As a general rule the equipment should be up and running and ready to use half an hour before the service starts.

In addition the worship must be prepared first and foremost, and then the effective use of technology can be explored. In other words, technology should be fitted around the worship, not the worship fitted around the technology.

This chapter starts the process by outlining a few simple things that should be done to enable this to be as effective as possible. The guides here are particularly helpful to those considering buying such equipment and using it in worship.

i) Projection

Projection is a helpful tool in a church. It easily allows images and text, especially for hymns and songs, to be made available to a large congregation. It encourages people to look up whilst singing which improves the sound. Projection can also be used for liturgy, notices, prayers, responses, quotations and also for images (as discussed earlier in the previous chapter).

There are two main types of projector, OHP (Overhead Projector) and LCD (Liquid Crystal Display) or data projector as they are sometimes called. Each have their advantages and disadvantages as follows:

OHP

Advantages over an LCD projector:

- They are relatively cheap to purchase.

- They are relatively easy to set up and use.

- You can change the order of slides very easily.

- They can be very bright on a good screen. This is particularly true for 450 watt models.

- They are easy to operate.

However, there are one or two disadvantages:

- The slides can be expensive to produce, particularly if colour images are to be used.

- It can be quite difficult to get rid of parallax (the distortion of the image where the top is wider than the bottom).

- Changing slides is a manual process and can be awkward.

LCD Projector

These have the following advantages over an OHP:

- It is possible to use larger characters and display one verse at a time.

- Coloured backgrounds can be used.

- Movement can be introduced onto the slides.

- The slides do not have to be physically produced and so are effectively without cost.

- All LCD projectors can be linked to a video or DVD player to produce high quality video.

- Sound and music can be linked to the slides.

- Changing slides is a very smooth operation as long as everything is in the correct order.

- The preacher/worship leader and choir can be given their own monitor to see what is on the screen without having to look around.

But there are disadvantages too:

- The initial capital outlay is huge.

- It can be awkward to change the order of slides if the worship leader/preacher changes things around (newer versions of software cope with this much better).

- There will be a need to develop new skills to produce slides.

Before we look at these two in some detail it is worth noting just a few general points.

The type and positioning of the screen is very important. The screen should be at a good height. In churches particularly it should be in a position where it can be seen from every position in the church. You can guess that if there are a few seats where it is hidden by a pillar one of those seats will be someone's favourite place. I have run an event in a large church where this could only be achieved by having two screens and two projectors. In addition monitors could be used to cover odd corners, choir stalls etc. It is possible to purchase break-out boxes that allow a video signal to be taken from a computer monitor output.

The screen needs to be positioned where there is no light shining directly upon it. Check where the sun will be for your service times, seeing how the light falls in the church and position the screen accordingly. The quality of projection depends as much on the screen as on the projector.

It is important that the amount of light falling on the screen is minimised. No amount of power in the brightness of a projector can compensate for the poor contrast you will get if light is falling on a badly positioned screen. Try the screen in different positions and see how dark it looks (perhaps even borrowing an old-fashioned light meter from a photographer). Then find out where any light is coming from and try to eliminate it.

There are also different types of screen. Unless you can completely black out a church (which probably isn't desirable anyway) consider a daylight screen. The screen area is covered with tiny pellets which reflect the light back out into the congregation. They work in a very similar way to reflective road signs and number plates and are very effective. They are not generally much more expensive than a standard screen. However, these screens do reduce the light levels for people who are seated at very oblique angles to the screen and are consequently looking at the screen almost from side-on, though this should not happen very often in churches.

Finally, no matter how well you position the screen there will also be someone who claims that they cannot read it — maybe more on principle than in reality, so when using the screen for hymns and liturgy make sure that you also have a few printed copies of the words available.

Look at the Premises section of the next chapter for advice on lighting and electrical sockets.

ii) OHP projectors

Overhead projectors have been around for a long time. They use a large transparency on a flat surface and the image on the transparency is projected onto the screen. They are easy to use and relatively cheap to purchase and maintain.

They generally come in two brightnesses, 250 and 400 watt (I have seen ones higher than that, but they are difficult to obtain). As the wattage increases the image will be brighter but the projector and replacement bulbs will be more expensive. On the whole it is probably best for churches to go for the higher wattage to aid visibility in buildings that generally have a lot of ambient light.

An OHP is essentially a box with a bright bulb within it cooled by a fan. A condenser lens distributes the light evenly onto a glass plate where the transparency is placed, and a second lens and a mirror on an arm above the glass plate focuses and reflects the image onto the screen. A focus control on this arm allows the focus to be adjusted. Some models also have a control for the condenser lens that allows you to adjust the consistency of the light on the glass plate. The arm may well fold down to ease storage and portability.

Portable OHPs are also available. The bulb is in the head at the end of the arm and instead of a box there is a plate with a Fresnell mirror on it. This is a mirror with circular grooves cut into it and it works as both a mirror and a lens. The transparency is placed on this mirror and the image is then reflected and focused onto the screen in the same way as the conventional OHP. This design has two advantages. The first is that when the arm is folded down it is extremely light and compact, making it easy to carry (it may come with a purpose-built carrying case). The second is that the bulb may not need a fan to cool it and so it is completely silent which is a huge advantage for churches. These models are probably more expensive to buy and the bulbs will almost certainly be more expensive. To balance this, in my experience, they are more reliable. Mine, which has travelled all over the world suffering from baggage handlers, is still going strong after nearly 20 years. If your projector is to be shared by several churches then it is probably worth considering a portable OHP.

To use an OHP properly you will need a stand for it. The higher the projector the less parallax (that is the widening of the image as you go up the screen) will be shown on the screen. Parallax can also be corrected by angling the screen forward. However, if it is too high then it will be awkward to position slides onto the projector. I would guess that the glass plate needs to be about four feet off the ground. If you are going to use the projector in different locations a stand with wheels would be a good idea.

A good tip is to use the mirror to align the top of the glass plate with the top of the screen in such a way that the slide is centred on the plate. Perhaps you could mark this position on the surround, but most certainly not on the glass! This means that the next slide can always be placed at exactly the right place and prevent the 'hunting' for the right place that you so often see.

The key to using an OHP well is in the quality of the slides. These must be clear and easily readable. Be very cautious about using colour as this can make slides difficult to read. The best combination is generally black on a blank or slightly tinted background. Only write slides by hand if your handwriting is very clear and has something special to offer. In other words, only do this if you are an expert calligrapher or have one in the congregation.

Slides can be made easily on a PC and either photocopied or printed onto slides. Be careful to use a large clear font. Arial at 36-point appears to be a good choice. Never photocopy the words straight from a song book on to a slide. This practice will not produce clearly readable slides, will discourage congregations from using an OHP, and also contravenes copyright rules.

Do not be afraid to add images to a slide as long as they do not distract from the words or reduce the readability.

Slides can be made in three ways and you will need to use the right kind of film in each case:

Write-on slides

- These can be written on using the correct marker pens.

- The pens used can be either permanent or wipe-off, though I have never found reusing slides to be totally successful.

- These must never be used in a photocopier as they will melt and damage the copier.

- If used in an ink-jet printer the ink will not stick and it will make a mess.

Photocopied

- These are made out of a special material that can withstand the heat when they are put through a photocopier.

- Slides can be prepared on a computer, printed onto paper and then copied onto the slide in a photocopier.

- This method can only be used to produce monochrome slides.

- Some photocopiers need a version of the film with a white strip on the edge to convince them that there is paper in the feeder tray.

- You can still use marker pens on them.

- If used in an ink-jet printer the ink will not stick and it will make a mess.

- This type of slide can usually be used in laser printers.

Ink-jet printer slides

- These are made from special material that absorbs the ink from ink-jet printers.

- You must ensure that they are loaded so that the printer prints on the rough side of the film.

- Some printers will need a version of the film with a white strip on the edge to convince them that there is paper in the feeder tray.

- These can be used to print in full colour.

- They can also be used for photographs, but always use the best settings on your printer and give the ink time to dry before touching it.

- The ink may run if they get even slightly damp.

- You can still use marker pens on them.

- These must never be used in a photocopier as they will melt and damage the copier.

- The slides are extremely expensive.

Each type of film has its purpose and use and they should not be interchanged. Each type should be kept in its box to prevent muddles.

It is easy to use a normal word processor to produce overhead slides. Note that if you are producing monochrome slides it is considerably cheaper to print on paper and then photocopy it onto a slide than to use an ink-jet printer. If using an ink-jet printer it is probably a good idea to make a test print on paper first as mistakes can be very expensive.

When slides have been produced and used it is a good idea to keep them organised and indexed in a file. The best way to do this is to use transparent pockets in a large Lever-arch file.

Remember that in order to project the words of hymns in this way you need a copyright licence and you need to record which hymns you have used. Perhaps the paperwork could be kept in the same file as the slides.

iii) LCD projectors

Video projectors have been around for some time – I can remember using a monochrome one during the mid-1980s. It was heavy, expensive and not very bright.

The first generation of colour projectors had three lenses, once each for red, green and blue. The colours were mixed on the screen. This meant that the screen had to be an exact distance away from the projector and each lens had to be perfectly in alignment. They were heavy, expensive and difficult to set up, which meant that they were not really portable. This type of model is still in use in some large conference centres.

The breakthrough came with single lens colour projectors. In these the light is still split into its constituent parts (red, green and blue) to go through three different LCDs, but it is reunited before passing through the main lens. This meant that they were easier to set up and were just about portable. They were still extremely heavy, outrageously expensive, and the bulbs cost around £400 and only lasted for around 600 hours. The light output was also very low.

My first projector was such a model. I had put the word out that I would like one and one night someone turned up on my doorstep and said, 'My company is getting rid of this, would you like it?' After lugging

it around for a few weeks I could see why they were keen to get rid of it.

As is always the case with technology, LCD projectors have become smaller, cheaper and better. Modern ones can be as small as a dictionary, can be bought for less than £1,000 and are considerably brighter than earlier models. The replacement bulbs are still extremely expensive (probably no cheaper than the earlier models), but many now last for around 6,000 hours, which actually, for church use, is probably the life of the projector.

Most projectors are capable of taking input from either a computer, usually either a PC or an Apple, or from a video signal, such as from a video recorder or DVD player. If you are an Apple Mac user, it is worth checking if a projector can accept video from your Mac. There will be a way (often labelled 'Mode') of switching between these. Some projectors allow for more than one input of each type.

There are a few technical points you need to be familiar with before you buy one. The first is the resolution. The picture is made up of thousands of tiny dots of light. The more dots (pixels) there are then the clearer the image will be on the screen. The number of dots across and down measures the resolution of the projector. There are essentially three resolutions available:

VGA

◆ These are 640 by 480 pixels and are generally acceptable as long as the image is not enlarged too much.

- This format is now not normally available, except in domestic models which are just coming onto the market.

- You would only come across it in second-hand machines.

- You may have to switch down the resolution of your computer screen to use a VGA projector.

SVGA

- These are 800 by 600 pixels which gives a reasonable picture in most situations.

- They are certainly fine for church use.

- If you are working on a limited budget then go for higher brightness rather than higher resolution.

- They can usually handle VGA and XVGA signals and will make the appropriate scaling for the screen, though you may find that it has reduced the resolution on your computer.

XVGA

- These are 1024 by 768 pixels and will give high-quality, sharp clear images.

- They match the resolution of a modern laptop.

- They can usually handle VGA and SVGA signals and will make the appropriate scaling for the screen.

The brightness of an LCD projector is measured in lumens. The higher the number of lumens the brighter the image will be on the screen. Churches present quite a number of problems for projectors as in most churches it is difficult to achieve a total blackout. This means that it is not an easy environment for an LCD projector and so the brightness of the projector has to be higher to compensate for the amount of light in the building.

Showing video needs more brightness than displaying words of hymns etc. This is because when displaying text you have control of the colours and brightness and can set them to have a high contrast. On a video these are set by the producer of the film, and night-time or low-light scenes can disappear altogether if there is not enough contrast between the darkness of the screen and the brightness of the projector.

Even with text you should always check colour combinations on the projector itself as they can look very different on the computer screen.

This is a rough guideline to what can be done with different levels of brightness, but the only way to be really sure is to ask the vendor to come and demonstrate the equipment in your church with your screen in the usual position. If you do this make sure it is in the daytime.

Brightness	Text	Video
700-800 lumens (recently refurbished machines)	This is generally OK for use in churches, except in an extremely light church on a bright sunny day. Blanking out windows nearest the screen and careful choice of colours may make the image acceptable. A higher rating is usually more acceptable in a church setting.	Low light and night-time scenes will disappear on bright days unless you have cut down the ambient light with a blackout.
1200 lumens (lowest available these days)	This is OK in many churches unless it is a bright sunny day.	These still would have problems with low light and night-time scenes on bright days without some blackout.
2500 lumens (mid-range)	This is excellent in all situations, except where sunlight falls directly on the screen.	There are still problems with low-light and night-time scenes if light falls directly on the screen.
3600 lumens (getting expensive now)	This is excellent and could be used even in large churches.	This is excellent in all church situations.

For most churches a 1200-2000 lumens projector would be generally acceptable. It would be satisfactory for projecting words in nearly all situations in the church and perhaps could be used for video in the hall using some blackout. If you want to show a video in daylight then you will almost certainly need something a bit brighter.

There are essentially two ways of installing an LCD projector in a church: permanent and temporary. If the projector is to be used only in one location, then it is probably best to use a permanent installation. The projector can be ceiling-mounted on a pole coming down from the ceiling. It is turned upside down to achieve this, so do ensure that the image can be flipped horizontally to correct for this. The projector will also need a remote control so that you can turn it on and off, adjust the brightness, contrast, zoom and focus (although in a permanent installation these should rarely need adjusting). The projector should be placed well out of reach to make theft difficult. The screen too can be wall-mounted as long as this can be achieved in the right position for the projector and congregation without it becoming intrusive.

In some circumstances it may be better to rear project. Rear projection screens are somewhat more expensive, but it is possible to purchase ones that increase the light output. The distance required behind the screen can be halved by using a large mirror, which can also be used to correct for parallax. Unless you are using a mirror in this way you should ensure that your projector is capable of mirroring the image so that it appears the right way round on the screen.

If the projector is going to be used in several locations, a temporary installation is required. The projector should be kept in a safe location and then brought and set up each time it is used. In such circumstances it would be wise to ensure that the projector has a carrying case (I have always found a padded soft case to be sufficient) and to use a sturdy stand for the projector and laptop. The stand for the projector should be at least 1.5 metres high to minimise the parallax that occurs when the projector has to be angled to reach the screen. They are expensive, but Unicol stands are excellent for this purpose and sometimes can be purchased quite reasonably second-hand.

When you are budgeting for an LCD projector, remember that you will need a computer to drive it. If you opt for a permanent set-up, then probably the best option would be a desktop computer (laptops are more expensive and extremely easy to steal). If you are only using the projector to display the words of hymns etc. and also some background images, then it does not need to be very fast, or have huge memory, or have a massive hard disk. The minimal configuration is all that is necessary. Do not let the salesperson sell you more than you need, but be sure to buy the best you can. You could certainly look at getting a factory-refurbished model.

The one useful addition is probably the ability to drive two monitors simultaneously. This allows the operator to adjust the sequence of the slides, call up new songs etc. without affecting what is on the main screen. This can be achieved either by installing a second video card or using a video-out connector or card. A second video card can be purchased quite cheaply, but some thought has to be given to the length of the cable run. Cable runs can be much longer using a TV video signal, but there will be loss of quality and contrast – not least because video is at a lower resolution and standard than a computer monitor.

It may be worth buying a machine with a DVD drive if you intend to show films on the projector. It is also possible to project video clips from a computer. If you intend doing either of these it is probably worth buying a machine to a higher specification.

If your church has a sound desk, then the obvious place for the computer is right next to it and then it is easy to connect the computer's headphone socket or line-out connection to the sound desk. Be very careful about using long cable runs between your computer and projector and check Health and Safety regulations regarding cables. Always check that all the plugs are firmly connected and minimise the possibility of someone tripping over the leads.

There are on the market a number of UHF wireless video connectors. At first glance they seem to be a good idea. I have experimented with them, but found them to be most unsatisfactory. The quality of the image is low and they are unreliable, subject to interference and adversely affected when people move around near them.

If you have a temporary arrangement and are transporting the equipment to different locations then a laptop is the ideal solution. As with desktops, if you are only using it to display words and images, then a minimal specification is all that is required. Ensure that the laptop has an external monitor socket for the projector and if it has a video-out connector then this is a bonus. If you wish to run DVDs and/or video then you will need a higher specification and if you wish to run video underneath text you will need a very high specification. The purchase of a soft carrying case and a cable-type lock is essential.

Please note that many laptops these days have a video-out socket as well as an external monitor socket and the LCD screen. However, do not assume that the laptop can drive all three simultaneously. Many laptops do not allow the external monitor socket and video-out to be driven at the same time. Check this out with the salesperson and, better still, see it working before parting with your money if you wish to use both external monitors and video-out simultaneously.

Note that the computer power required to run a video clip or DVD on two video screens simultaneously (i.e. on the computer's own screen and the projector) is considerably more than is needed to run the same on one screen. If you have problems trying to run video on your projector, turn off the main computer screen by hitting the right mouse key on the wallpaper and selecting 'Properties' and then 'Settings'.

Unfortunately the speakers in computers and projectors are somewhat small and tinny and the sound produced when showing a DVD or video is in no way commensurate with the quality of the picture. This can be dealt with either by linking the sound from the computer or video player to the church's sound system or by buying a reasonable combo amp to use with the projector. It is better to use a 'keyboard', rather than a 'guitar', combo amp as the latter can distort the sound.

You should try to avoid projecting up at a steep angle as the image will be distorted (wider at the top than at the bottom). However, many modern projectors have a 'Keystone' facility which allows you to compensate for this. If you know this is likely to be a problem then, when you purchase, look for a projector with this 'Keystone' facility. This can work in different ways on different models and on some projectors using it will result in jagged edges or part of the image missing.

Many projectors come with a remote control. This, in most cases, can be used to zoom and focus, blank and turn the projector on and off. In addition the remote control usually can be used to drive the computer and the presentation. There will probably be a serial, control or USB port on the back of your projector. This is designed to be connected to a serial, mouse or USB port on the PC and then the projector will use its remote control to simulate a PC mouse. This means that the presentation on the PC can be driven from the projector's remote control. It would be helpful to check out your documentation for this useful feature.

The Family Friendly Churches Web Site[1] contains the words of many 'out of copyright' hymns as PowerPoint™ files. These can be downloaded and saved by using the right mouse button and than they can be quickly built into PowerPoint™ displays by using 'Insert' and then 'Slides as File ...'

Do remember always to shut the projector down in the proper way and never simply switch it off at the mains, unless you enjoy buying expensive bulbs.

You will also need to purchase (or download) projection software to permit the computer to make a presentation. This is covered in the next section.

And remember, a few pounds extra spent on a screen and lighting may save hundreds in projectors.

iv) Projection software

You will then need software to drive the projector. The most used software for this is Microsoft PowerPoint™, but there are other choices that may be worth considering:

Microsoft PowerPoint™

This is very easy and fun to use. It has proved to be very reliable and I have never known it crash during a presentation. It has a great range of effects and transitions (changing slides). The easiest way to learn it is to simply load and play with it. Look carefully at Backgrounds, Custom Animation and Slide Transitions. It is acknowledged (sometimes grudgingly) to be the best as well as the market leader. It is very reliable and is also compatible with other Microsoft software. PowerPoint™ is part of Microsoft Office XP. Microsoft offers discounts to charities and those involved in education, though do check your entitlement before you buy.

If you have a worship leader who likes to change the order of songs, or plucks songs out of the air (or from the Holy Spirit) then you will need PowerPoint™ 2000/2 or XP with twin-screen handling. This will allow you to change the order of the slides without affecting what appears on the screen. It is a very useful facility.

My guess is that whatever software you decide to use you will at some time need to buy PowerPoint™ as it is the most common presentation software on the market, and so many people find themselves buying it simply to be compatible with others.

Impress

This is part of the Open Office Suite of programs which is a set of free software roughly equivalent to Microsoft Office 97.

Impress is the display manager part of this and it is also roughly equivalent to PowerPoint™ 97. It functions very like PowerPoint™, has a good range of backgrounds, graphics, animations and transitions and can read and write PowerPoint™ files – although Impress does not always interpret PowerPoint™ animations and timings accurately. However, it does not have twin-screen handling so can be awkward if you wish to change the order of slides during a presentation.

Impress can be downloaded from Open Office[2],but note it is a 50Mbyte download so you will either need Broadband or a long time and a reliable connection!

Specific song packages

There are a number of packages that have been written specifically to handle songs, such as 'Songpro' or 'Presentation Manager'.

These contain a large library of songs, hymns, Bible versions and backgrounds built in. This can save a lot of work and assures freedom from copyright issues for the user, and in addition they do allow you to add your own hymns to the library. These, of course, will not be covered for copyright.

These generally do not have the number of effects and transitions of PowerPoint™ and generally offer very little flexibility as to how the words will appear on the screen. However, they do allow you to call up a new hymn without affecting the display of the current hymn and they also have added facilities like the ability to post a message on the bottom of the screen. They can usually read, control and display PowerPoint™ files as part of their presentation.

This type of software will generally assume that you have access to dual screen working and a separate operator.

You can find out more about 'Presentation Manager' at Sunrise Software[3], and about 'Songpro' at DM Music.[4]

Visual Liturgy

Visual Liturgy is a package for producing liturgy quickly for a service. It has built, in the text of the liturgy, the words of many hymns and the lectionary readings from the Bible. It understands the lectionary and will very rapidly compile the elements needed for a service. It can then either print these out or allow the user to copy and paste the resulting liturgy into any other documents or presentations by either PowerPoint™ or Impress.[5]

v) Using technology for music

Increasingly in small churches it is difficult, if not impossible, to find musicians who can play week by week. Sometimes a musician can be found who will play some of the time or will play some of the music, but is not able and/or willing to play the full range that a family friendly church requires.

Modern technology can help in this. It is currently not (and probably never will be) as good as a competent musician playing a fine instrument, but it is probably as good as many churches can currently muster.

There are essentially two solutions:

Using CDs or tape

Advantages:

+ CD and tape players can be purchased quite cheaply, though good ones are more expensive.

+ They are simple to operate and people are used to operating them at home.

+ CDs and tapes of hymns and worship songs are readily available.

Disadvantages:

+ The CDs may work out to be expensive when you think how few songs can be fitted onto one CD.

+ What you hear is what you get. The tempo, pitch, levels and instrumentation cannot be changed to suit a congregation.

+ It is difficult to make good quality recordings onto tape or CD.

+ Tapes are less suitable because they can be very difficult to cue up in exactly the right place.

Using a MIDI instrument

Advantages:

+ The pitch, tempo, levels and instrumentation can all be changed to suit the congregation.

+ Many non-copyrighted tunes are available on the internet. Very often they are free of charge.

+ MIDI files can easily be recorded on a keyboard or organ that is equipped with a floppy disk.

Disadvantages:

+ The capital equipment cost is slightly higher.

+ It is slightly more difficult to use than a CD player.

+ You will probably need access to a computer and someone in the congregation with the skills to handle the technology, though the disks could be built by someone who is not a member of the church.

CDs and tapes have been around for a long time. Both systems save the sound that the instruments make through a microphone. Sound is saved on a tape as a series of analogue levels on a magnetic tape, but CDs convert the sound into digital values and then place these onto a reflective surface. This means that CDs give a better quality of reproduction.

Saving sound requires huge amounts of data and so will need either a lot of magnetic tape or space on hard disk or CD. Stereo sound at CD quality uses around a megabyte for each ten seconds of sound. This means that the sound files are difficult to move around and cannot be downloaded from the internet.

This is why the performance is fixed as it was recorded with no flexibility in tempo, pitch or instrumentation.

MIDI was originally an interface for connecting electronic instruments together so that one keyboard could be used to control other instruments. Later on the interface was used to connect musical instruments to computers.

In more recent times floppy disks have been added to keyboards, initially allowing a musician to save tunes and styles. Today these floppy disks can also be used to move MIDI files from keyboards to computers and vice-versa. In most cases the floppy disks on a keyboard are completely compatible with those on a PC. In addition most modern PCs can also play MIDI files without being connected to a musical instrument at all.

MIDI is totally different to tape or CD. These save the sound that has been generated, but MIDI saves what the musician does, such as which instruments are selected, which styles are selected, which keys are pressed and with what velocity. These instructions are transmitted from the keyboard and passed onto either another musical instrument, a PC, or written by the keyboard directly onto a floppy disk.

The files produced in this way are very much smaller than those used on a CD. This means that they can be stored very easily on floppy disk, which may be able to save up to 50 MIDI hymns. In addition MIDI files can be downloaded very quickly from the internet as they are so small.

However, this means that the complete performance is not fixed, but rather is regenerated every time it is played. The result is that it will sound a little different on each kind of keyboard and computer.

The advantage of this is that the instrumentation, levels, pitch and tempo can all be changed as the music is being regenerated. It is this flexibility that makes MIDI superior for leading worship.

There are a number of different ways of buying and using MIDI in worship. Each way has its advantages and disadvantages as follows:

Dedicated MIDI box

An off-the-shelf packaged unit that plays MIDI files. It will usually come complete with a floppy disk drive, control panel, amplifier and speaker.

Advantages:

- This is a very easy way of getting into MIDI. You should be able to buy it, plug it in and it should work.

- It is relatively cheap.

- It will probably come complete with a set of disks containing MIDI files of a number of popular hymns.

- More MIDI files will generally be available from the supplier or from the internet.

Disadvantages:

- It is dedicated to the task of playing MIDI files and so has no keyboard, which means it cannot function as an organ for the times when a musician is available.

◆ It cannot record MIDI files if you wish to create your own library of MIDI tunes.

The organ that plays itself

This is a fully functional organ which is sold complete with a full set of MIDI disks containing around 500 of the tunes used in *Hymns & Psalms*. The tunes are played by a very skilled musician and have the right number of verses for *Hymns & Psalms*. There is a keyboard option available which is somewhat cheaper. This system is supplied by David Cooper.[6]

Advantages:

◆ The system is sold as a package, complete with a large library of MIDI recordings of hymns.

◆ A number of modern worship songs which are in copyright are also included.

◆ It can be used as an organ when a musician is available.

◆ You can record your own MIDI files.

◆ The quality of the musicianship and sound is very high.

◆ You still have the option of getting MIDI files from other sources, such as the internet.

◆ The organ (but not the keyboard) comes with personal installation and instruction.

◆ The quality of the musicianship is high and visitors to a church using this have sometimes been taken aback to discover there was no organist!

Disadvantages:

◆ It is a relatively pricey way of solving the problem.

◆ There is a keyboard option at a much lower price, but it does not have the range of instruments and styles that are available on many modern keyboards.

Organ with an add-on box

If your existing organ or keyboard has a MIDI port you can buy an add-on floppy disk player that will allow you to play MIDI files.

Advantages:

◆ This uses your existing organ or keyboard.

◆ It is a very cheap solution.

◆ The instrument can still be used when a musician is available.

◆ You are free to get the MIDI files from wherever you wish.

Disadvantages:

◆ It is possible that you may not be able to use this to record your own MIDI files, so you will need to check this before purchasing.

◆ Your existing instrument does need to have a MIDI-port available. Only relatively modern organs will have one, though most keyboards will probably have one.

◆ You will have to purchase or download MIDI files.

The PC alone

Most modern PCs can play MIDI files without any need for them to be connected to a keyboard or organ at all.

Advantages:

- There is no need to purchase a musical instrument.

- It is easy to download MIDI files from the internet directly onto the computer and build a library of tunes.

- There is no need to use floppy disks.

- If the computer is a laptop, it is very easy to carry from one location to another.

Disadvantages:

- PC speakers are extremely small and tinny, so you will need extra amplification.

- You cannot make your own MIDI files as there is no keyboard, but you can generate them from the music (this is very laborious).

- Computers were not built to generate sound as their primary function and so do not sound as good as a dedicated MIDI instrument.

- You will have to purchase or download MIDI files.

A keyboard

These days keyboards are real instruments and not the toys they used to be. They work very well with MIDI files as they are the instrument that MIDI was designed for.

Advantages:

- Modern keyboards offer a great range of styles and sound.

- Nearly all of them have a built-in MIDI interface.

- Many have floppy disk drives built in.

- Many have a Direct Connection built in (see below).

- They have a good sound if played as an organ.

- They can very easily record MIDI files.

- They are relatively cheap to buy.

- They are easily carried from one church to another.

- In the hands of a skilled player a keyboard can sound like a whole orchestra.

Disadvantages:

- In a large church a keyboard may need extra amplification.

- You will have to purchase or download MIDI files.

- There are different types (mappings) of MIDI files. For instance, a MIDI file designed for a Yamaha keyboard will probably not work properly on a Roland.

Having purchased a MIDI instrument it is necessary to get the music from your computer to the organ or keyboard. There are three different ways of doing this, each with its advantages and disadvantages as follows:

Full MIDI Interface

This is using the interface in its full form.

Advantages

* This method will allow you to connect almost any MIDI instrument to your computer.

* Allows you to 'daisy chain' multiple instruments so the computer can control several instruments.

* This method will give you full MIDI capability.

Disadvantages:

* You may well need to buy extra hardware for your computer.

* In addition you may need to buy extra software, a MIDI driver.

* It can be very difficult to get everything working; you really do need to understand how MIDI works.

* It may be hard and expensive to find this hardware for a laptop PC, although it is now possible to buy a USB to MIDI cable, which may well be useful for all computers.

Extra Equipment

You will probably need to purchase:

* A sound card with a joystick/MIDI interface.

* A MIDI cable.

* The correct software driver for your MIDI instrument.

Direct Connection

Many keyboards now have a Direct Connection port which allows connection to a PC's serial port (or even USB).

Advantages:

* It is easier to set up and usually connects to the serial port or USB port of a PC.

* It can be bought as one package from your keyboard supplier.

* It can be used on a laptop, though you need to check carefully that your laptop, or any you intend to purchase, has the correct connection.

Disadvantages:

* Each different keyboard will have its own standard.

* You cannot assume that there is any compatibility between different keyboards, even between two different models made by the same manufacturer.

* It can still be difficult to load the software and get it fully working.

Extra Equipment

You will probably need to purchase:

* Cable, software and drivers which will be available from your keyboard supplier.

Floppy Disk

Many keyboards now have a floppy disk drive, which is completely compatible with a floppy disk drive on a PC.

Advantages

- Generally the disks are in PC format so it is extremely easy to transfer music from PC to MIDI instrument.

- This is a very quick, easy and cheap way to use MIDI.

- You do not need to carry the computer to your church. All you need to take is the floppy disk.

- Tunes can be recorded on the floppy disk and then taken from the keyboard and copied onto a PC.

Disadvantages:

- Your keyboard must have a floppy disk drive installed.

Extra Equipment

You will probably need to purchase:

- A box of floppy disks.

- You can buy a stand-alone floppy drive for a keyboard as long as it has a MIDI port.

Having got a MIDI instrument and computer connected together and working you will need to build a library of MIDI files, unless they have been provided by the supplier of the equipment. However, even in that case, you will probably want to supplement what has been provided. There are three ways MIDI files can be obtained.

Create them yourself

In most cases you will be able to record MIDI files. There are two different ways of creating MIDI files:

1 – Get a musician to play them.

- You will need to find a competent musician to play the tunes, but it is quite possible that someone from another church may do this for you.

- Then you will need either a MIDI instrument that can record on floppy disk or one that is connected to a PC.

- You will be amazed how jittery even the most competent musician will become when you are recording them, so allow plenty of time for the recording sessions.

2 – Get a computer specialist to code them.

- This is done by coding the music into MIDI instructions and is a very time-consuming operation.

- The results should be note perfect, but very mechanical and musically sterile.

Purchase them

A number of companies sell pre-recorded MIDI files. These may come on CD, but it should be easy to transfer them to floppy disks.

Questions to ask before you buy:

- Are there any issues concerning copyright? Any copyright costs should be included in the licence.

- May I hear some samples first? After all, you may not like the arrangements.

- Have they been played by a musician or coded by a computer specialist? The second will be note perfect but musically sterile.

- Are they complete recordings, with an introduction, the right number of verses and a conclusion?

- How much do they cost? They may not be cheap; in fact, some of the prices could be described as exorbitant.

Download them

A number of sites have downloadable MIDI files of popular hymns and choruses.

Points to consider:

- You may well be breaking someone's copyright. This is less likely with traditional hymns, but most likely with modern worship songs.

- The quality of the musicianship in the recordings can be variable.

- Have they been played or coded?

- Are they complete, with an introduction, the right number of verses and a conclusion? Many tunes on the internet consist of just one verse of the tune and no introduction or conclusion.

If you are sure that a tune is out of copyright then it is most likely that you can download it from the internet. Strictly speaking, the performer of the music still has some copyright over the performance, but in most cases the fact that they have placed it on the internet expresses a desire to see the recording used as widely as possible. This is certainly the case with the Family Friendly Churches Web Site. In the case of other web sites it might be worth checking this either on the web site or by e-mailing the originator of the web site.

It is very easy to copy a MIDI file from a web site to either your hard disk or a floppy disk. Tunes can be played on most sites by pointing at the link and clicking with the left mouse button. To download a MIDI file, again point at the link, but click the right mouse button instead. A small menu should appear. Click on 'Save Target As ...' and the normal file Save menu will appear. Use this to select the desired folder (or floppy disk), give the file a name of your choosing and then click on 'Save'. It is a good idea to have a convention for names such as the number in your hymn book, the first line of the words or the name of the tune. In this way you can start to build a library of files.

Do check again that it has the right number of verses. If there are too many then the tune can be faded out at the appropriate moment. If there is just one verse then it can be used, but someone will have to restart it at the beginning of each verse. The tunes on websites that are linked to a specific hymn book, such as the Family Friendly Churches Web Site, will usually have the right number of verses for each hymn.

It is very easy to search the whole internet for MIDI files of just one specific hymn. Go to a search engine such as Yahoo or Google and if, say, you are searching for 'And can it be', type the following into the search box: 'And can it be' + MIDI, then hit 'Search'. You then should receive a list of MIDI-file web sites that contain 'And can it be'. You can then hit the links, listen to the different options, and download the one you like the most. Do remember that generally they will sound much better on a MIDI instrument than on a PC.

Generally MIDI files come organised into channels. Each channel represents a different instrument. Some may only use one or two of these channels, one web site uses a piano on channel one and something that sounds like a choir on channel two. Others use up to 16 channels, using some channels for drums and others for accompanying instruments. If a tune sounds odd then it may be because the playing instrument is not allocating the right instruments to the intended channels

(Apple Mac and Roland users need to be particularly aware of this). It is possible on most keyboards to reassign instruments to channels and to turn off channels that are not required.

It is not possible to cover how to do this in a book, because every model of keyboard is different. It is worth your spending time experimenting with your keyboard and finding out how to vary the tempo and pitch, how to turn different channels on and off, and how to set the level of each channel. As well as being the best way to learn, it is also great fun!

6

A look at the rest of the church

So far this book has focused very much on worship. It is right that it has done so, for worship is the heart of all that we do, but there are other aspects to church life as well. This chapter seeks to explore how these can be made family friendly. Remember as you read this that family friendly is much more about fostering an attitude of mind than just creating a list of events.

i) Premises

People so often refer to the building as a witness, and indeed it can be, but are you sure it is a good witness? If the building looks uncared for, dilapidated, tatty, unwelcoming and cold, what sort of witness does it give? What does it say about our attitude to God, if we are prepared to let his house get into such a state?

I was once the minister of a village church, where I visited a couple wanting their child baptised. After the discussion they asked me where the Methodist Church was and when I told them they replied; 'Oh, there! I thought it was closed.' How are we going to draw people into a church if the local community believes it is closed already?

Keeping a church in good order is so important. Inside and out, the maintenance must be done, not only because it keeps the rain out, but also because it speaks volumes about the approach and attitudes of the people who worship there. People can pick up the signs given out by a poorly maintained building very easily and will give the place a very wide berth.

We assume that people understand that they are welcome to come into a church whenever they wish. This is far from the truth. I remember a few years back preparing for a youth service, when an arm appeared around the door and beckoned me outside. There on the outside was one of my youth club girls with her friend, whom I did not know. The one I knew asked: 'Is it OK if my friend comes to the service?' In another church on my visits a young woman told her story. She lived opposite the church, but went to the parish church quite a way away, as she was not sure whether she was allowed to go into the Methodist Church across the road. During a bad winter when travel was hard, she wanted to take a look, wandered across the road and met someone who showed her around and reassured her that she was welcome. He had managed to do what the church buildings had failed to do.

Although we cannot erect a neon flashing light above the church that says 'Everyone welcome, including you, Mrs Jones', we can do things that signal to strangers that they would be welcome.

The first is to have a clear access. There was a church where I served that had a huge hedge surrounding it. The church had been very attractively refurbished, with an open foyer so that people could see right through into the church – or would if it wasn't for the hedge. I persuaded them to cut down the hedge. Within weeks a number of people living in the area said to me, 'Oh, it's a church, we always wondered what was hiding away behind the hedge.'

I think people assume that buildings like this are some kind of secret society, which is not surprising when so many churches still give no view of the inside to the outside world. So the first stage is to open up your church so that people can see in. Remove hedges, fences, gates and anything else that gives out the feeling that the building is not a place that anyone can just walk into.

Some churches, like the one above, are worried about security. They used to get wound up over local folk who used the car park as a short cut. Why? This isn't a problem. It's an opportunity. A strategically placed notice-board can have an impact, and security is actually reduced if you have a high hedge and gates, because once someone is over the gate, then they can proceed with their activities at leisure with no danger of being seen. It is much better for security and mission to have the approach to your church as unimpeded as possible and, even better, to use plenty of glass so that people can see inside and see what happens in there. They will then find it much easier to walk into the building when the time is right.

Then there is the inside. Why is it that so many people like all the modern comforts and conveniences in their own homes, but like their church to be locked into the nineteenth century? The truth is that there is nothing more off-putting to outsiders than pews, bare wooden floors, out-of-date heating systems, high pulpits etc. People may have admired the place if they have been to a wedding or baptism there, but it is in the sense that people admire a museum, not as an active and relevant place to meet God. Despite what they say such people rarely come back the following week.

In days gone by people tried hard to make their churches at least as comfortable as their homes, and usually much more comfortable. As we have made our homes more and more comfortable our churches have got horribly left behind, and now most churches are viewed as cold and uncomfortable places. The attitudes behind this need to be addressed.

In the village churches of my current circuit there is compelling evidence of the importance of keeping churches in good order with modern furnishings. All the village churches in the circuit that have refused to modernise, and have hung on to their traditional look, have either closed or are in serious trouble. This is in contrast with those that have undertaken some modernisation, in most cases removing the pews, carpeting the floor and buying some modern chairs, which have either held their own or are growing. One in particular was on the point of closure a few years ago. It had a refurbishment and is now a healthy church with a regular congregation which fills up to two-thirds of the building. Refurbishment of the church buildings isn't a magic wand. It will not turn a church around on its own, but in my experience it is a vital first step if you wish to draw new families and young people into the life of your church and want to see it growing once more.

Most important of these, in my opinion, is the removal of the pews. On the whole pews not only give a church an outdated look, but they are usually uncomfortable and make the building inflexible. A building crammed with pews cannot be used for any other purpose but Sunday worship and perhaps the occasional concert, whereas a building with chairs can be used for a host of activities. One village church in my current circuit had the pews stripped out about two years ago and is now using the space gained to run, with the neighbouring Anglican Church, a weekly club for about a dozen children in the village. They also have been able to host meals, for example, the Harvest Supper, in ways and numbers that they could only have dreamed of in the past. This is work that would have been impossible in a building still with pews and because of this work this little village church is slowly coming back to life.

Chairs also offer flexibility in layout that pews cannot. You can, if you wish, place them in a circle, or a horseshoe shape, or side on, or around the edge, or even use no chairs at all. You can also put out just enough chairs for the numbers of people you expect. Pews force you to one format and usually to the long thin layout which, in my opinion, is the least appropriate for worship. They also permit members of the congregation to sit scattered around a large building, which is always disastrous for worship.

In most churches with pews the only free space is at the front. This means that if a little one chooses to wander (and no force on earth can stop a two or three year old from wandering) then the only place they have to go is right at the front. This is in everyone's sight lines and is very distracting for some older members of the congregation. My experience is that, where chairs are used in such a way that there is space at the side and back of the congregation, children, instead of wandering forward, tend to wander to the side and back.

Couple this with the simple provision of quiet toys at the back, perhaps in a play-house as at '10 to 10' in Cromer or a children's chapel as at Wiveton, and the problem of wandering toddlers will, on the whole, be solved.

In many churches there is another reason why toddlers wander towards the front. So many traditional churches have rails, a pulpit with steps and a table. Try and become a three year old again, look at all of that, and imagine what are you going to think. You are going to think 'Whoopee! A playground!' To a three year old it looks just like a modern adventure play area. No wonder they are drawn to it all like a magnet and start clambering up the steps. If you have all this at the front of your church, consider losing it all. A church doesn't need all that as much as it needs those toddlers and their parents. At the very minimum it would make sense to close off this area with stair gates.

There are other reasons for getting rid of it all. The Disability Discrimination Act (DDA) is making a huge difference to churches and it is not just about installing new toilets. If it has a pulpit with steps a church cannot say to a preacher, 'You must use the pulpit', for that would be discriminatory against those who cannot use the steps. Every church is having to make provision for preachers to preach from floor level. If a church has a sound system and a loop, then this should include provision of a microphone at floor level. If you have to make all this provision and as preachers seem less inclined to use pulpits these days, then perhaps the time has come to remove all this paraphernalia at the front of so many of our churches.

The DDA is making churches look at access to their buildings and tackle the issue of any stairs and steps that are in the building. As a church considers wheelchair access then it should also consider access and parking for pushchairs and buggies. In providing toilet facilities, then it should also look at baby changing facilities. So many of these issues go hand in hand.

One of these issues is the seating of wheelchair-bound people. If a church has chairs then a chair or two can be removed to allow for a disabled person (or a child in a buggy) to be seated in the body of the congregation. Where a church has pews then a wheelchair-bound person or a child in a buggy is nearly always left sticking out into an aisle. After she suffered a stroke my mother-in-law was wheelchair-bound. She found sitting in her wheelchair in the aisle very embarrassing. Here is yet another good reason to get rid of pews, but if a church insists on keeping them, then please, please, do cut back some of the pews by about a metre so that a wheelchair or buggy can be accommodated in the body of the congregation. Heartsease Lane Methodist Church has done this successfully, though they have done it at the back. I have a feeling that it would be best done through the length of the church, say, every second row on alternate sides.

Do remember that where a church has a sound system and a loop, again because of the DDA, it must be used. The days when preachers could get away with saying, 'I don't need a microphone' are very nearly over. Remember to have microphones positioned at all the places where sermons may be preached or lessons read etc. Each church must have someone who knows how to operate and check the equipment (including the loop) and all preachers must be microphone trained. All that is done in this area will not only help a church be friendlier to those members of its family who have hearing impairment, but also be helpful to families. There is no doubt that good use of a sound system can help overcome many of the difficulties that arise from the voices of small children during worship.

The Disability Discrimination Act is not there to prevent the able-bodied from doing things. It is designed to enable people with disabilities to participate as far as they are able. For example, it doesn't prevent us from projecting the words of a hymn on the screen, providing the words are also provided on paper for those who find looking at a screen difficult. We can use dance and movement as part of our worship as long as we are creative in how we encourage those who find standing and moving hard.

The Act is quite clear that we do not have to change the nature of our worship to accommodate people with disabilities, although we have to do our best to include them in what is happening. This will require some creativity and flexibility on everyone's part. My experience is that this is what people with disabilities want. For example, my blind colleague, the priest of the local Anglican church, makes good use of the data projector installed in his church and most certainly hates being guided around like 'the blind man'. I recently watched a performance where one of the chorus was blind and was gently guided around the stage. I studied alongside a student who, despite being wheelchair-bound, was a pretty mean table tennis player. With determination on their part and flexibility on our part there is very little that a disabled person cannot achieve. More information on the Act can be found on the internet.[1]

Finally, think about colours. A really big issue! I have spent hours in meetings arguing about colours. The wrong colour scheme can really damage the atmosphere of the church. Children like bold, bright colours. The head teacher of a local primary school painted all the internal doors a different bold bright colour and the children loved it. Go for warm colours, reds and pinks rather than cold greens and blues. Get rid of any dark stained wood around the walls. Nothing makes a church look more out of date than this. At the very least strip it and varnish it in a much lighter hue. Do all you can to make the building light, bright and airy, whilst remembering the previous section on positioning and using projection screens.

Don't forget about the procedures for your church. Anglicans will need to obtain a faculty from their bishop, Methodists will need to talk to the Property Division at Manchester. I have always found the authorities helpful and supportive if you involve them early on in a project.

If you have the opportunity to refurbish the lighting, look at using spot lamps to create very controlled directional lighting. I have done this in a village church, placing 32 spot lights in the ceiling, controlled in banks of four by dimmer switches. This allows the lighting to be controlled very precisely. It is very helpful for churches that regularly use projection. Even within the confines of this very small chapel it is possible to light the congregation well enough to read a hymn book without difficulty, whilst keeping the screen dark enough to give really excellent contrast.

Whilst on electrical matters remember, if you get the opportunity, to position a power socket in the floor at about the point where the projector will be (at least a double, and if using LCD projection, probably a quadruple socket). We did this in the above church and it has proved most useful; it also eliminates dangerous trailing cables, which must be covered if you have them. If you are using both OHP and LCD projection then position the sockets halfway between the two. Don't try to guess the position, but get them out of the cupboard and make sure the positioning is right.

ii) Structuring children's work

Many of the churches I have visited have said roughly the same thing about the nature of their children's work, although perhaps in different ways. Essentially they have talked about 'Fun', 'Friendship' and 'Jesus'.

Before we look at these three, there is one element that is central to all that we do with children. That is 'security'. All that we do must ensure that the children who come to us are kept safe and sound. This means that we must take very seriously all the issues that surround child protection matters. If a child is harmed in any way whilst in our care then we have failed that child and all the work we have strived to initiate may disintegrate. The topic of security is discussed in the next chapter and is a matter of great importance. The other elements, 'Fun', 'Friendship' and 'Jesus', rest on this.

'Fun' – The days when parents pushed unwilling children through the door into Sunday school are long since over. If you want children in your church you have to win them, for there are plenty of other things for them to do on a Sunday morning! The only way children will come is if they want to come and so what you do has to be enjoyable for them. It has to compete with sport, or TV, or the internet, or the cinema, all things that they could be doing instead. So what you do has to be fun. This doesn't mean that you have to compete on the same terms as all those things, because the truth is that children still enjoy some of the old-fashioned stuff. My experience is that games always go well. One of the most successful games I have introduced to different groups was 'fish racing', paper fish flipped along the floor with newspapers – it has been around for years. Children also still enjoy making things, such as cutting, sticking and pasting. Interesting craft is a winner and I have found the most successful craft is cooking (though this needs loads of safeguards). These are things that many children will not be able to do at home or on the internet etc., and so this gives them a new fun experience. We have laid on internet access for one of my kids' groups, but to be honest they are much happier playing games, running around and making things.

'Friendship' – Here we can offer something to a child that virtually no other activity can give. That is the time and genuine interest of an adult. So many children are starved of this. Parents are often very busy (and, anyway, they are parents and don't count as people in a child's mind), teachers are stretched to the limit and cannot give time to individual children. Here in a church group a trusting relationship can develop between child and neutral adult. Ideally here is someone who can listen, support, help and give a child that most precious of commodities: time. In the structuring of the work, do give time in small groups and do encourage these relationships to grow. Some churches use buddy systems (where children are paired up with church 'parents' or 'grandparents') to encourage this to happen.

'Jesus' – And then to the reason why the work is done. We want the children to meet, know and then love Jesus. Too often the work has been seen in terms of teaching children the Bible or about Jesus. The idea of this is that if you teach children about Jesus they will become followers. It works occasionally, but the best way is for them to get to know the living risen Jesus for themselves. Clearly, teaching about the Bible and teaching children about the Jesus who lived in history is an important part of the process, but more important than this is teaching them how to develop a spiritual life that will help them meet with the spirit of the living Jesus.

I have always had a great concern for those adults who troop out with the children week after week. The demise of evening worship often means that those who lead in a Sunday school get very little opportunity for worship and teaching of their own. In addition to this it can separate the Sunday school from the church and produce two groups with very different outlooks on what the church should be doing. I have seen these splits quite often and suspect that here is the root cause.

I have found people in their 30s still going out with the Sunday school and they have known nothing else. They grew up in the Sunday school and when they were about 16 or 17 they became helpers and then later leaders. I knew a couple in one of my previous churches who were in exactly that situation.

I have come across Sunday school leaders who have been worn out by the process. They have been leading for years and Sunday by Sunday they are always giving out and rarely receiving anything in. Because of this they have dried up and have lost the vision they originally had. Some of them would like to give up, but feel that they cannot because there is no one willing to make the same commitment. And so they plod on without energy or inspiration. Quite frankly, people in such a position are doing neither themselves nor the children they serve any good at all.

London Rd Methodist Church in King's Lynn has tackled this problem and appointed three teams of leaders to work in the Sunday school (known as The Zone). There are three superintendents each with a team of people. Each team usually leads for three weeks, from one all-age service to the next. This means on average that each person is leading for three weeks out of 12 and they are free to worship in the body of the congregation for the other nine weeks. Clearly there is some flexibility here and swapping between teams when a person cannot make a particular Sunday.

The main advantage is that no one is wearing themselves down by going out week after week. Each leader continues to be able to be part of an adult congregation for the majority of the time and is able to worship and receive teaching and encouragement on a regular basis. There is less division between the main service and Sunday school because the leaders are still part of the worshipping congregation.

Clearly a much larger team of volunteers is needed, but the experience at London Rd was that people were much more willing to come forward knowing that they would not be expected to lead every week. Although the other stated dis-advantage is that continuity is lost, for London Rd the continuity comes from the material and style of The Zone, and the children and young people seem quite able to cope easily with a variety of leaders. Since the new system was applied The Zone has continued to grow.

The matching of leaders to age groups is very important. I have seen mismatches in the past where the personality of the leader did not match the needs of the particular age group. In one case a change of age group for one woman gave a whole new lease of life to her long Sunday school career. Unfortunately in another case, the whole business ended up with a messy resignation.

The needs of each age group in a Sunday school are completely different. When these needs are understood, then the appropriate leaders can be appointed.

The children of crèche age (0-3) need a gentle and safe environment. They can be given some toys to play with and perhaps be led in some gentle games and a song or

two. Above all they need to feel secure and that mum and dad are not too far away and will return. Indeed, this can be a good preparation for the days when such separation will happen. My two children went quite happily to nursery school and I am sure that time in the church crèche helped in this. In this day and age nappy changing is probably achieved best by fetching a parent out of the service. A parent may need to stay with an upset child at times, so it can be a good idea to relay the service into the crèche.

The leaders need to be gentle people with a love of small children and babies, who can provide this loving, calm and safe environment. They need also to be people who can win the trust and support of nervous and anxious parents. It is rare that a child creates a fuss for long after a parent has left them and so the leaders need to reassure the parents of this and persuade them to bring and leave their children as quickly as possible. It is vital that you have a crèche on standby, even if you have no children of this age, so that it can be swung into action at a moment's notice when it is needed.

By the time children are 4-5 then they are ready to start receiving some simple Christian teaching. They still need a gentle and kind environment, but alongside the play there could now be some simple storytelling, some games and songs. The leaders need to have skills in storytelling and be able to lead a song or two, still in a kindly and safe atmosphere.

Children of 6-7 have by this time settled into school, are used to some structure and now have an increased attention span. They will be able to start doing some craft activities, such as cutting, colouring and pasting. They will need a lot of help and in many cases it is worth having much of the preparation done. Stories, now perhaps with some simple explanations, will be important and some simple songs may also be part of the programme. The leaders still need to be gentle and kind, but now with some practical and creative skills.

Children of 8-10 have totally different needs. Here the emphasis needs to be on excitement and fun. Their sessions should be loud, lively and energetic. There should be some games, loud and energetic action songs and perhaps some drama that they could take part in. Craft activities can still be used with this age group, but these children are now becoming competitive, so games and quizzes will always go down well. This is also an age group that is technologically aware. They will have mobile phones, computers, games consoles and so on, and all of this will influence their behaviour and language. This age group can generally read well enough to gain information on their own behalf, but may be more willing to read a computer screen or the internet than from the Bible.

Their leaders should be out and out extroverts, who can share a joke, tell a slightly rude story, leap about, make fools of themselves, wear silly clothes and largely join in the fun. In addition they need to be familiar with technology and where appropriate use it to present the case for the gospel and Jesus.

In my experience young people of 11-14 are the most challenging age group. They are experiencing many changes. Their schooling has changed from primary to secondary and suddenly they are the little ones again. Before they have got used to this their bodies start to change as they become adults. Their hormones begin to rage. Generally for this age group the opposite sex is becoming no longer something to despise, but something in which to take a great deal of interest. This is a great problem for them as they have no idea how to deal with the opposite sex. In many ways this group is torn in two. They are still children and like doing childish things, like craft etc., but at the same time despise it as childish.

This group, above all the others, needs to have the right leaders. They need people who can lead them as they start to explore all kinds of philosophies, who are broad enough to listen to all sorts of ideas without saying that any are wrong, but at the same time gently nudging them back onto the right path. The best leaders are those who will listen as they explore and give gentle guidance, without saying that a way or belief is wrong, but gently showing the inconsistencies. They need leaders who are quite content to lay aside a whole week's preparation because suddenly a different issue has come to the fore and no topic should be out of bounds. Sometimes one question from a group member can throw a whole session and has to be explored by the group. These leaders need to be able to talk about sex and sexuality honestly and openly and without getting embarrassed, for this is the big issue for this group. In addition such leaders need to be able to let group members at times be children, and do children's things, without making them feel childish. A really good way of achieving this is to let them 'help' the younger ones.

Young people of over 15 need to be active and involved. Those in this age group have developed skills and can be amazingly talented in music, art, drama and dance. They have much to give and they want to contribute. By this time they will be entering into relationships and getting hurt when they break down, or not getting into relationships and being hurt because they feel undesirable. Some will be capable of leading a service, providing music for worship, giving a talk or a testimony, putting together a dance in worship or creating artwork as part of worship. This group has immense technical awareness. They can work sound desks, computers and video projectors with ease. Radio Cookham, an RSL radio station run by the churches in that village, depended on young people who had finished their GCSEs to operate the station technically and they were brilliant at it! They are also, once more, becoming politically aware and do not have the scepticism that older people have. They recognise injustice and they want to campaign against it, and they believe that they can make a difference.

Leaders for this age group need to be good motivators and able to get them out doing things using the amazing talents that they have. They need to be able to help young people to prepare worship etc. without imposing their ideas upon the group. When the youngsters go one idea too far, the leaders need to defend them from the rest of the church. When they want to campaign on an issue, these leaders need the abilities to show them how to do this, how to make a press release, how to make some kind of protest, how to handle journalists and a radio interview (the MAYC World Action Campaigns are always sources of good material here[2]). In a world increasingly media dominated, these are skills young people need to develop. All this needs to be coupled with showing them how to develop a devotional and spiritual life and giving them the skills to defend their Christianity and it must be done in a way that deepens commitment to Jesus Christ. They will need these skills when they go to university (and, be assured, if they do all the above, they will go to university!).

Although this section has talked about different age ranges these are only guidelines and the age ranges have fuzzy edges. There are natural age boundaries between groups of children and young people and we must be careful to work with these rather than against them. We must recognise these within each individual Sunday school. One of the worst things we can do is put up a whole natural group from one class to another and then leave one child behind, because his or her birthday is in September rather than August. The one left behind may only be a month younger than others who have gone up, but is now left behind with a group they perceive as being much younger.

Thinking that they have been abandoned, they will quickly become discouraged and may even stop coming. At the very minimum we must learn to show real flexibility when moving children from one group to another and recognise natural boundaries and friendships.

However, much better than this is to move away altogether from the whole idea of moving children up and to move leaders to groups. In other words it is better to recognise the natural boundaries that exist within a group of children and to keep these groups together and, when they need a change in the style and type of leadership, then bring the new leaders to the group. In this way a church is working with the natural friendships and groupings that happen among the children rather than against them.

iii) All-age events

In an earlier section I explored how churches have broken the generations apart, by focusing on separate activities for the different ages. I believe that this has done much damage to churches and the time has come to correct this by including all ages in the events that are happening in the church life.

In most churches the generations have become disconnected and this is the root cause of many of the tensions in traditional churches today. This can only be corrected by encouraging the generations to mix in a social and fun setting, so that relationships across the age range can once more be built up.

Not everything that a church does should be serious and earnest. There is nothing wrong with having social events that are designed to build up relationships within the church family as long as that is not all that a church does.

There are a number of events in the year when the church family comes together to celebrate. One of these, for example, is the Harvest Supper. Try and persuade the organisers to think what will attract all ages to this. What sort of food is right for such a wide age range? How should we sit? Is there a way we can encourage the generations to sit together at one table and share? So often, either the children are all put together on one table with, perhaps, one poor unfortunate adult, or we sit just in families or with our particular circle of friends. Try and find ways of breaking these things down.

Then there is the entertainment. Try and make this appeal to all ages. So often we just default to a speaker, who may, but more likely may not, be able to hold the children's attention. Perhaps there could be a film or video shown or a game or quiz of some sort that everyone could join in.

There are a number of trading games available that give people a chance to experience in miniature the injustices of the trading system in the world. It would be easy to use these in an all-age situation and to mix the teams so that they were multi-generational.

Why not use a quiz? It is a really fun way of learning. If the quiz were to involve hunting around for things, then children could be fully involved, or in each round have a couple of questions specifically for children so that it becomes a positive advantage to have a child in a team.

Although some may shudder at the prospect of Family Fun Days, they do have a role to play, in allowing the generations to mix in an informal atmosphere. If you have sports, please do not allow people to cheat. This can really upset some children and sends out the wrong signals. If you are playing competitive sports, do not even cheat to even up the scores. It is a much better lesson for life to ensure that the winners are magnanimous in victory and the losers are gracious in defeat.

Drama is a really good tool for mixing the generations. Somehow this is an art that appeals to all ages. The age differences are laid aside as everyone, from the youngest to the oldest, prepares for a performance. In one of my churches the biennial pantomime (and that's probably often enough) was a real treat. The youngest performers were just seven or eight and the oldest were in their 80s. However, one has to be careful not to let this become a tradition and dominate the life of the church.

I would suggest that every church takes time to look at its social church calendar and try to place within it events that are multi-generational and will bring the generations together in a way that they have to co-operate and work together. It would be very beneficial to see churches moving away from a pattern that separated out the generations and working on activities that would reunite them.

iv) Helping parents

Bringing up children is an extremely difficult task, probably the most challenging thing that anyone can take on. Nurturing children in the Christian faith is also difficult and children are at the receiving end of much that discourages them from committing themselves to, and following, the Christian way.

At school they can experience some considerable taunting about their faith, and not just from children. Unfortunately, and shamefully, it is our personal experience that teachers can indulge in this activity too. These days much can mitigate against church attendance for children, with not only sport taking place on Sunday, but with schools often having rehearsals for plays and concerts on a Sunday morning, with a three-line whip being applied for attendance.

The role and example of parents is vital if children and young people are to be nurtured in the Christian faith. It is my experience that the deeper the commitment of the parents the more likely it is that their children will grow into committed young Christians. Children soon pick up on any faith or commitment that is shallow. Unfortunately they will nearly always respond at the level of the least committed parent. I have noticed in all my years of experience of working with children and young people that, generally, (and there are exceptions – I'm one myself) children from homes where both parents are fully committed to Jesus are those most likely to commit themselves. Conversely my experience is that in households where one parent is very committed and the other is not, the child tends to follow the path of the less committed parent.

Parents need all the help and support that they can get from the church. This is why it is so wrong for church members to criticise parents when their children do not behave as well as they would expect. Such criticism is always wounding to parents who are doing their best to nurture their children in the Christian faith. This is even true if the comments are gentle and good humoured. Parents know when their children are causing a disruption. They are generally more sensitive to their children's behaviour than anyone else and are deeply embarrassed by it. Any comment, even well-meaning, will often trigger a response that is more violent and damaging than the comment means or deserves. More families have walked from churches over comments made by the congregation than for any other reason. The only safe policy is to grit your teeth and be patient and understanding.

When people complain about the conduct of the children they are nearly always thinking of a group of two or three year olds. In my experience there is no power on earth that can keep them still. So remind yourself that in the future that 2 year old who is wandering around causing mayhem now will possibly be a delightful 5 year old, an energetic and enthusiastic 10 year old, a challenging and thoughtful 14 year old and a deeply committed 18 year old. All that can be put at risk by an ill-judged comment to the parents at this time.

If children present a challenge to a church, then the church needs to thank God for the presence of these children and then rise to the challenge. If a baby is crying, then perhaps what that mother needs is someone to offer to take the child for her, or perhaps the church needs to organise a crèche. If toddlers are wandering around, then perhaps the church needs to look at its layout and use of furniture, or its provision for small children. Maybe the church now needs to make provision for a Sunday school or to adopt strategies for all-age worship.

Parents will not keep coming to a church for long where all they do is sit outside looking after their own children. They might as well do that at home. I heard of a church which recently invited a group of mothers and children to a Mothering Sunday service. They were sent out with their own children, where they were expected to make their own Mothering Sunday present and then extra ones for the ladies of the congregation. Is that any way to treat guests?

Parents also need help and advice as to how they can nurture their children in the faith. Parenting courses can help in this. There is plenty of material available for these. There are also courses that can be used to help non-church families in parenting. I have heard stories of these providing not only a service to the community, but also a bridge to help families to start being part of a church.

Above all, though, parents need help in the task of nurturing their children to become young Christian men and women. This is a difficult and complex skill and parents need help, training and support in how to do it. I suspect that most families do not pray or study the Bible together and, again, this is a challenge to which the churches should try to rise.

Another area to examine is that of house groups, study groups or cells. Whilst some churches run cell groups for children and teenagers, is this again splitting the age groups? Are there ways we can make these multi-generational? Is it possible that a large multi-generational house group could meet; all tackle the same issue, but perhaps separately for a while before coming together to share across the ages? In all of this can adults learn to value the insights of children?

Finally, can parents be given an occasional break from their children? I heard recently of a church that ran a Valentine's evening for all its younger married couples. The church organised babysitters and provided a meal in the most romantic atmosphere that is possible in a church hall. I am told that the gesture was very much appreciated by these couples. I believe that this is a wonderful way of saying that we appreciate the task they are doing in nurturing the next generation of Christian men and women.

v) Employing lay families' workers

There is now a tendency for churches to employ a lay families' worker or lay pastoral assistants with a focus on families.

This is a move I would welcome on the whole, but I believe that great care must be taken for there are, I suspect, some dangers in doing this.

There is a great temptation for church members to feel that, now there is a professional doing the work, there is no longer any need for them to volunteer. I have seen that happen with lay youth workers. A church I worked alongside appointed a youth worker a few years ago. Within a few months many of those who worked with young people took the opportunity to jump ship. In time this damaged, rather than enhanced, the youth work in that church.

I feel that there is a danger of the same thing happening following the appointment of a lay families' worker. This can be avoided by making it clear that, with the appointment of a professional, the work with families should grow and this will need more volunteers, not less. If the congregations are not prepared for this then the appointment should not take place.

A second temptation is to overestimate grossly the amount that one person can achieve. I have seen the job specifications for some families' workers and they border on fantasy. They are far too broad, cover far too many churches and are generally too vague. The specification needs to be narrow and specific.

If someone is to be appointed then they need to be targeted at specific churches that are capable of supporting the work that the lay worker does. A good test of the right churches would be those which have signed the Family Friendly Charter and are working towards making their worship family friendly. A major premise of this book is that if this is not being done then there is little point in pouring resources into work with children, teenagers and families. This would include the appointment of a professional families' worker.

Do also remember that if the appointment is part-time then the amount that can be achieved is reduced and this should be reflected in the job specification. A full-time worker can probably work effectively alongside two churches, a part-time worker alongside one. A worker would also need probably two or three years to make an impact, even if the church is fully playing its part.

vi) Other suggestions

This really is just a list of ideas that I have applied or seen applied.

If your church has a rota for cleaning, flowers, stewarding, reading, etc., then for some of the entries, with their permission, put the name of a family who can work together on that particular task. Children and young people like to be included in this way.

An idea I have seen applied in some churches is one of church grandparents. Many children these days live a long way away from grandparents and see them only occasionally. The converse is also true for many of the older generation. Why not offer those who are willing to be honorary grandparents to individual children within the church? Such 'grandparents' will have to be cleared through child protection clearance procedures, such as 'Safeguarding Children'. Safeguarding is covered in more detail in the next chapter.

How can we give pastoral support to children? It is a fallacy to suggest that all of childhood is idyllic. There are many traumas associated with growing up and I have already suggested that Christian children can get a bumpy ride at school. Surely it is wise and valuable to find ways of giving pastoral support to our children. Perhaps this could be coupled with some kind of membership scheme that allocates them their own visitor, who does indeed visit them and gets to know them (subject to their parents' permission and presence and the rules of 'Safeguarding Children'). This is nothing new. I have often heard people talk of Sunday school teachers who in the past were also diligent visitors of the children. In this way they got to know not only the children but also their families. This can be a really good way of showing that we care.

Most children and teenagers do not keep diaries and haven't a clue what they are doing in two days' time, let alone a month away. Getting publicity into their hands and then into their heads is a major problem. In my experience it is better to put a small flyer into their hands rather than to put a poster onto the wall. For families this needs to be in really good time. I think my family is typical. For all of us to be free on the same evening is a rarity and certainly needs to be planned several months in advance.

I have found that e-mail is the best way of communicating with the children and young people in my church groups. It is very easy to build a mailing list of all their addresses and then a reminder e-mail can be sent in a few minutes to the whole group. I even include the parental permission slip on the e-mail; they print it out and get the respective parent to sign it. Nearly all the members of my groups have access to e-mail and I ask those who have email to print out the document and pass it on at school to those who don't. This seems to happen fairly reliably. It is possible even to send text reminders to their mobile phones, perhaps just a couple of hours before an event starts. Certainly I have found text to be a good way of communicating with teenagers and you don't need to learn 'text language' to use it. They do seem to be able to read and respond to everyday English!

7

Bringing about the changes

i) Start with worship

Let us assume that you have read all of the above and you would like your church to be family friendly. You are probably feeling a bit bombarded with ideas and are wondering where to start.

There is a great temptation to start the task by introducing some kind of children's work, perhaps a holiday club, midweek club or by kick-starting the Sunday school. Providing you can find the leaders this is a nice easy first step and providing nothing is broken, or the walls aren't written on, you will not get too many complaints about it.

However, to do this would be merely repeating the errors of the past and so my earnest desire is that churches will resist this temptation and start by reforming their Sunday worship to make it family friendly.

Earlier on I hinted that it was not a good thing to continue to divide families as we have in the past so that Sunday worship is seen as an adult activity or, even worse, an elderly adult activity. Too often in the past churches have started and run very successful children's and teenagers' work, but have not allowed this to impact on what happens during Sunday worship. I accept that very successful work can be done and is being done in children's and teenagers' groups and, indeed, children and young people can feel very welcome at these separate groups. But it is not enough to welcome them just in their own groups during the week. This welcome must extend to worship on a Sunday, otherwise we are not giving them the best we can.

This limited welcome is far too common. It was why so many of the 'Pacesetters' fell by the wayside. It is why I have discovered in churches couples of around 35 who have never actually worshipped in the body of their congregation. They grew up in the Sunday school, became junior helpers, later they became leaders and somewhere along the line they met up and married. In all of this they never made the step from Sunday school to joining the full worshipping body of the church and now, quite possibly, they have children of their own in the Sunday school.

Churches must learn to take a much more holistic view of what they are trying to do. The more I study and reflect upon being family friendly the more I have come to realise that it is not about 'doing', but rather much more about 'being'.

Family friendly isn't about activities, it is about attitudes.

So, if you have a youth group meeting now on your premises, ask yourself the question: if the youngsters we have in the group came along to church on a Sunday morning, what would happen? Would they receive a warm welcome? Would there be some part of the service that would be relevant to their background? Would they be made to feel out of place, because they didn't know when to stand and sit or which book was which? What would happen, if they were not perfectly quiet and well behaved?

Unless you can give positive answers to these questions and have strategies for dealing with this scenario then your children's and young people's work will largely be a waste of time. Ask their leaders: 'Would you be totally comfortable to invite the children and young people whom you lead to worship on a Sunday?' If the answer is 'no', then ask for reasons why and absorb and act upon the responses. In many senses children's and young people's work in a church that does not have family friendly worship is a road to nowhere for the children and young people involved.

I see this so often. During my sabbatical I visited a good friend who is running a number of successful clubs for children in a Methodist circuit in the north of England. She is a fine practitioner at all levels and can draw children into these clubs and lead them to make a commitment to Jesus. She can link this work to older youth clubs that keep the children on church premises. But unless there is a commitment by the rest of churches to change their worship so that it becomes attractive and relevant to these children, young people and their families, that is all she is doing – keeping children and young people on church premises.

Before you start any such work you should face the possibility that the children, young people and their families concerned may want to worship with you. Examine your worship carefully and ask yourselves, as a church: 'Are we prepared for that?' If the answer is 'no', then work on that before you start the children's or youth work.

Doing this may be helpful in other ways. Most families when they move into an area will try out the local churches. Their first contact with you will most likely be during Sunday worship. For them Sunday worship is like your shop window and the church is judged by how it is conducted. It is also the point where many other families will have their first contact with you, not just those who have moved into the area, but perhaps those who have been invited to a baptism; or a wedding couple who are looking for a church and who have been invited along as it has been suggested that this may be helpful for the big day; or a couple whose first child has just become three and they feel it would be a good idea for him/her to join a Sunday school. All these things do happen and in most cases if they do not like what they see during that one Sunday they will move on and look at another church. A church has just one chance to get it right for each family.

ii) Managing change

Have you heard the one about, 'How many Methodists/Anglicans/Baptists does it take to change a light bulb?' 'CHANGE!!??'

Let's face it: it is not easy to make changes in a church. There are those who will resist change at all costs. I suspect that many people have seen so much change in their working and home lives that they are left feeling confused and muddled. After all, some of our older people remember days when motor cars were a novelty, when they communicated by letter and huddled around a radio for entertainment. This generation has seen change at an unprecedented level and I suspect that for some their church is a source of stability that is not found anywhere else. And, of course, God and the gospel message are unchangeable, although the ways we understand and express them will change.

And, whilst this is true, it is also true that our understanding of God grows and develops as the Spirit leads us into new truths. While the gospel message is as true and straightforward as it was when Paul wrote his letters, the way we communicate that gospel message has to be in tune with the lives people are leading now – Paul knew this when he was in Athens and adjusted his presentation of the gospel to meet the culture he was trying to reach.

The mistake that some people make is that they want their stability to be built upon how we worship – the hymns, liturgy, language and styles of worship, rather than what they worship, the essential unchanging nature of God, or why they worship, because of the unchanging gospel message. Sadly, this mistake has meant that they have built their house upon the sand, for the way we worship cannot remain constant. They have sung, 'For nothing changes here' meaning their church rather than their God.

Ultimately churches that simply become a comfort zone for people, rather than a place where people are challenged by the gospel coupled with an expectation that lives will be transformed, are always sitting on the verge of extinction. This is not 'change for change's sake' but change to keep the church engaged in its mission.

For such people changing the way they worship is a massive threat to the stability of the church. Some would rather see the church close as their generation dies out than see change. The attitude of 'This place will see me out' is not uncommon in our churches and somehow such people need to be gently led to see where their true stability is.

I think there are three main stages to this process. The first stage is to explore the nature of the problem and to explore whether the Family Friendly Charter is part of the solution for your church. The second is then to do the Family Friendly Audit and to decide upon the changes that are needed. The third stage is to implement the changes. The first part of this will almost inevitably involve some consultation with other parties and groups.

However, first and foremost commit yourselves as individuals and as a church to pray about this. Set regular prayer times in church. Give people prayer diaries etc. that they can use in their personal prayers. All the following processes should be built upon prayer, and don't forget to leave times to listen to God and to hear his guidance.

iii) Exploring the problem

People, first and foremost, need to see the need for change. Time must be taken to explain why change is necessary. It is only through lengthy and patient explanation of what is happening to our churches that many people will come on board and start to see the need for the changes that must be made.

The meetings that discuss these points must be open to all who are part of the church. It is not enough for a minister or priest and a few stewards or wardens to try to force these changes through. It is less than ideal to use a Church Council, for this too is still limited. If you really want people to support the process, then the consultation should be as wide as possible.

The first chapter of this book is a good tool to use to get over what has happened to the churches over the last 40 years. People are aware of the problem of declining congregations and missing generations, but it does help to see the bigger picture. The figures are essentially Methodist, but my guess is that these figures are echoed in all the major traditional denominations.

The first chapter also explains the knock-on effect of the decline and how this has left us short of volunteers, finance and ministers, and having explored the depth and seriousness of the problem it tries to explain the causes. If this material is used then great care should be taken not to point the finger at individuals, as they will become defensive and that will damage the outcome of the meeting. However, it is vital that everyone understands the serious nature of the problems that the traditional churches face and the consequences of not tackling these problems.

There will be a need to explore how the national situation is being reflected in the local situation. There will be those in almost every church who can remember times when there were a host of children, young people and families. Encourage people to talk about this, perhaps even showing photographs from those days. It might be a good idea to ask people to think how they would tackle this problem. Perhaps buzz groups could be used to do this.

This is probably the moment to introduce the Family Friendly Charter. Time should be taken to explain to everyone that adopting the charter will mean that there will have to be changes. It will have an impact on the Sunday-by-Sunday, day-by-day, week-by-week life of the church. It may be that some treasured objects and customs have to go. Emphasise that the whole tone of the charter is that worship is at the heart of the church and this is where the changes must be made first.

As part of the discussion here it might be useful to study one of the case studies that are available. There is a wide range of churches and situations among the case studies and so there is a good chance that there will be at least one that is relevant to your current situation.

The CD-ROM contains a PowerPoint™ presentation of the figures, graphs and main points covered in Chapter 1 along with slides covering the Family Friendly Charter. If you have access to data projection these may be very useful in giving this presentation. The case studies are also found on the CD-ROM as both a detailed HTML file and a set of abbreviated PowerPoint™ slides. These can also be used for the presentation. The Family Friendly Charter is also available as a Word file and that may be used to give everyone a copy of the Charter.

Always remember that at this stage the aim is to ensure that everyone makes an informed choice, knowing and under-standing that changes will occur as a result of acceptance. It is not simply to get the charter signed at any cost.

iv) The Family Friendly Audit

The next stage is to work through the Family Friendly Audit. This is probably best done by a small group. The group should represent all aspects of the church's life. This may be covered by the stewards' meeting, but I suspect in many cases they will want to co-opt others to ensure that the breadth of church life is covered.

The audit covers three aspects of church life: Worship, Activity and Premises. The main aim of the audit is to let a church explore whether in these areas the needs of all age groups are being held in some kind of balance. For the purpose of the audit a congregation is broken into four rough areas: children, young people, parents and grandparents. The lines between these groups are rough-and-ready and always blurred. Parents and grandparents in this context are used to signify a rough age range, not whether people are actually parents or grandparents.

The form to guide a church through this process can be found on the CD-ROM in Word format. Feel free to print as many copies as you wish for this stage. As a group work through this form. You may need, as part of the process, to monitor a month's worship in the church and check the actual balances. You will need representatives from all the age groups to tell you whether the activity did actually hit the target age range.

When this has been done, there is space on the form to highlight where the group feels the greatest imbalances are. These should be agreed and then noted on the form. The result of the audit then needs to be made available to the whole cong-regation.

When this has been done the larger congregation should meet again to affirm the work of the group, accept the imbalances and then work through some aims that can put the imbalances right. Each part of church life needs to be looked at, but I believe that the priority is to sort any imbalances in the worshipping life first.

From this it should then be possible to map out some changes that you would like to make. Do not be overambitious in the plans that you make. Do not expect that you can plant an all-age congregation with hundreds of teenagers worshipping in a warehouse by next year.

Nearly every church leader I have interviewed has said that small changes in the direction of being family friendly have resulted in new children and families becoming part of the church family relatively quickly. This also matches my own experience in ministry where small changes to the worship in the first few minutes of a service when children and young people are present has quickly drawn new families to the church. Seeing the new people in the congregation encourages and builds the confidence of a church and makes future changes much easier. If a church already has a Sunday school then my guess is that changing that first few minutes when everyone is together is probably the most productive first step.

Do remember that the exercise is aimed at providing something for everyone in the church family. Do not make changes that go from one extreme, such as only catering for the grandparent generation, to another, such as only catering for teenagers. A church catering only for teenagers or children is no more family friendly than one catering only for older people.

In meetings try to get a consensus rather than a majority. Whenever there is a vote on a topic like this there will be winners and losers. Real and acceptable change cannot easily be made in such an atmosphere.

When you have made and agreed the plans then they can be written onto the Family Friendly Audit form, which then can be photocopied and sent off. Once registered a church can be listed in the Family Friendly Churches Web Site and is allowed to use the Family Friendly Church logo on its building and all publications and publicity material. After 12 months the audit form is sent back with a review document so that a church can review how the changes have been implemented and then set new targets for the next 12 months. Visitors are invited to use the Web Site to make comments and suggestions and these too will be forwarded to a church as part of the review.

Remember most of all that small changes can make a lot of difference. Some people will tell you the ways forward are to include building a bonfire and putting the traditional hymn book on the top, then recruiting the services of a worship band, handing the service over to the control of a worship leader and changing everything in one go. I beg to differ. I want change to be such that everyone can be kept on board. It is better to make a small change, review it, and then make another small change each year than to try to make a huge change in one go. This has worked well in many of the case study churches.

v) Consultation

It is almost certain that any proposed changes will affect other people and communities. It is therefore vital that these people and groups are consulted, have their views taken into account and hopefully are encouraged to be supportive of the changes.

I have placed these into four categories as follows: practitioners, authorities, other churches, and the local community.

Practitioners

The practitioners are those whose ministry will be directly affected by the changes and so it is vitally important that these individuals and groups are kept informed and encouraged to be supportive. Nothing makes an individual less inclined to support change than to feel that they have not been consulted.

These are the musicians, worship leaders, preachers and Sunday school leaders who play an active part in our worship.

If new music is to be introduced then the church musicians need to be at the heart of the process. It may be that for part of a service a worship band is to be used. It is vital that the musicians you wish to play are consulted about the level of commitment required for this (playing in a worship band every week is a huge commitment in terms of rehearsal and practice) and also the level of musicianship required. Not all musicians are comfortable with, or even capable of, playing all styles of music. Musicians who now play less must be reassured about the value of their ministry.

The preachers and worship leaders need to be consulted about any changes in the style of worship, particularly if the style is to be all-age. Not all preachers feel comfortable working with children or know enough of the new worship songs to work with them. If this is the case then a congregation must offer people from the church who can lead that part of the service for them. It was very noticeable that in nearly all cases the churches in the case studies had decided to lead the all-age part of worship themselves rather than rely on external preachers and worship leaders.

Sunday school leaders, too, should be consulted about any changes that will affect them. For instance, if children are to return from Sunday school back into church for Communion or a sharing time, then the leaders must be consulted, for it places restrictions upon their work.

Authorities

It is reasonable to assume that the minister of a church is at the heart of any process of change and most likely driving the pace of change. Indeed, if they are not fully supportive of the changes then I suspect that there will be problems to come.

However, there may well be other authorities that have to be consulted when making the changes. For Methodists this will almost certainly include a discussion with the local preachers' meeting. There are many preachers who take the view that they have the absolute right to lead worship in the way that they feel is best. In addition some local preachers feel challenged when asked to lead worship that includes modern music or is geared towards children, feeling that this is something they cannot do well. Any approach to the local preachers' meeting has to be made carefully and sensitively and the church is best placed if it can offer to help the preachers who struggle in these areas. Over the last few years much has been done to encourage churches to have a say and participate in the leadership of worship and so it is not unreasonable for a church to say to a preacher, 'If you cannot do this then we will.'

I am not talking about the preacher being merely a provider of entertainment, though the great preachers of the past were indeed great entertainers, but the role of the preacher and worship leader is to lead and participate in an act of worship that touches the whole congregation whatever the spread of ages, backgrounds, abilities etc.

This has been seen in nearly all the case study churches I have visited. The local church has decided on a style of worship and has said to preachers, 'This is what we want, if you cannot deliver it, we will do these parts for you.' I would venture to say that this level of involvement in worship is almost a requirement for a local church to become family friendly.

For Methodists, in addition, the support of the Superintendent Minister is key. They make the plan and so decide which preachers are sent to each church. If a church has the full support of the Superintendent Minister, then they can help by sending only those preachers who are in tune with the direction in which the church is going. This kind of support has also been very evident in the churches in the case studies.

My guess is that churches of other denominations will also have to consult widely in order to receive support from the structures in which they operate.

Other churches

Other churches in your area should also be consulted. In rural areas it may be that the only way that certain work can be done is ecumenically with other churches. In these cases it may be better to work jointly from the beginning. I have seen a children's club start in one of my own rural churches. This could be done only as a joint venture with the village parish church. This work is not only successful in drawing children into the church, but it is also drawing the two congregations closer together.

It has also been my experience that families do move to a family friendly church from other churches in the area. Whilst this should not be encouraged it is almost inevitable and this kind of movement has been seen in most of the case study churches. In fact, the case study churches show that families are prepared to travel some distance to worship in what they see as a suitable church. Therefore, it is wise to meet with other church leaders to assure them that poaching is not intended and that children and families will not be encouraged to move from one church to another.

The local community

It is also important to consult the local community. If you are planting a new church then it is desirable to know what the perceived local needs are. An important aid in this process could be a questionnaire. Certainly 'The Bridge' found this to be helpful in selecting the time, location and style of their work. The best way of conducting such a survey is to go house to house and fill in the forms as part of a conversation. If you rely on people to pick them off the doormat, complete them and return them, the vast majority of them will take the short journey from the doormat to the bin. Talking to people on the doorstep will allow you to explain your plans and to show them that you really are interested in them and what they would like. A questionnaire will prevent you from making mistakes of timing (say, running at the same time as a popular local event) or style (misjudging what people actually want). A copy of 'The Bridge' questionnaire can be found on the CD-ROM.

Contact with local schools is also important. Despite many horror stories circulating about head teachers not allowing Christians within three miles of their schools, I have always found head teachers to be more than willing to allow me to go into schools and to lead assemblies. My initial approach has been always to make contact with the head teacher and arrange to go into the school to discuss how I can help in assemblies. I have always assured head teachers that if they set any boundaries I will keep to them. If you are confident that your minister is/would be good at leading school assemblies then encourage them in this role. In my experience the most serious offence in leading an assembly is to be dull or boring. If you suspect that your minister might be either of those then gently discourage them from doing assemblies and find someone else, or even a team of people, who can do them well.

Part of the R.E. National Curriculum is to visit places of worship. Why not invite a class to come and visit your church? What I do for such visits is to label the various places and bits of furniture, produce a sort of 'I-spy' worksheet, and allow them to explore the church. Have the table set for Communion (if your theology can stand it with cola in the glasses) and the Bible on the lectern. If a youngster is learning the piano let them have a go on the organ and so on. Go through the sheet with them and invite them to ask questions. I have found that children (and teachers) really enjoy such a visit.

Publicity is a vital part in this consultation and is covered in a later section.

vi) Resources

As you prepare to make changes then you will need two types of resources, human and physical.

The next stage is probably to identify those who will be working with children face to face. In many churches people willing to work with children are somewhat scarce so you may need to look around for help. It may be possible to get help from neighbouring churches of the same denomination or a large town centre church could help a small village church restart work in this way. Or you could set up a circuit redevelopment group that will help individual churches kick-start new work with children. In rural areas it might be possible to work together with a church of a different denomination doing joint work with children.

Having identified those who will work with children there are then two essential steps. Everyone working with children in this way must be checked and cleared for the work. The processes laid out can be found in 'Safeguarding'.[1] As a minister who has had a paedophile try to infiltrate the children's work of one of my churches, I can vouch at first hand the importance of the systems and guidance laid down in this document.

The information below, a brief synopsis of 'Safeguarding', is designed to give you an idea of the level of bureaucracy now in place for the protection of children and young people and cannot be considered in any way as an alternative to buying a copy of 'Safeguarding' and implementing it in your church. No church can be exempt from the guidelines laid down by 'Safeguarding', not even those who have no children's work and haven't seen a child on the premises for last 15 years.

There now seems to be three levels of application:

1) Appointments requiring a Disclosure.

A Disclosure reveals information about a person held on the Police National Computer and other government databases. They have to complete a form and apply for a Disclosure of information. There is a small fee for doing this. These now should be done for all new appointments. There are two levels of Disclosure:

a. Enhanced Disclosure: The vast majority of children's and youth workers need this as it applies to those who are 'regularly caring for, training, supervising or being in sole charge' of children or young people.

b. Standard Disclosure: This is a very small group of people (compared to the above) who may come into contact with children and young people on church premises, but have no supervising or training responsibilities.

2) Appointments not requiring a Disclosure.

These are people whose position of responsibility may not necessarily bring them into contact with children, but that the position in itself carries some kind of responsibility for managing work with children. Those in these positions should sign a declaration that they have never been convicted of, or cautioned for, an offence against a child or young person, but a full disclosure is not required.

3) Other appointments not requiring a Disclosure.

This covers not only nearly all office holders in a church, but also key-holders, caretakers and mini-bus drivers. These need to sign a simple form that states they are aware of the policy on 'Safeguarding' and know of no reason why they cannot fulfil the office to which they are appointed.

The 'Safeguarding' booklet contains photocopiable forms for all the situations above and also has background information, guidelines for safeguarding children and information about recognising abuse and actions to take when it is suspected.

If you ever have the misfortune to have to report a case of abuse, then please remember that a number of people will need a lot of support. The young person concerned is about to have a very tough time. They may be removed from home and then required to give evidence which may be videoed. This is a frightening and unpleasant experience for a young person and will do them great harm. I have heard a minister describe reporting abuse against a young person as 'throwing them to the wolves' and this is not far from the truth. The young person concerned will need a massive amount of pastoral support and will need to be constantly reminded that they are precious and valuable and will not be forgotten – even if they are placed in a secure unit over 50 miles away and deliberately cut off from their friends.

If the young person belongs to a youth group then that group will also need a lot of support as they come to terms with what has happened and is still happening to their friend. They may have suspected that something has been going on, or perhaps have been told about the abuse by their friend, and will have feelings about not reporting it.

Parents of young people in the group exhibit a range of responses. These range from being willing to give the abused young person a foster home to seeking to distance their young person from the situation and the people involved. These parents, too, need help and support as they come to terms with what has happened to a young person in their social circle. They may even know and be friends with the alleged abuser.

Then there is the person who has reported the abuse. As they watch the young person 'go through the mill' they may feel guilty and wish they had never spoken out. They may well face threats from the abuser, who probably will be able to guess where the report has come from. This may result in threats of violence, or as I have faced, misuse of the church's disciplinary procedures.

Do not forget the family of the abuser. Their lives have been thrown into turmoil. Perhaps other children have been removed from home and will need reassurance and support. Then there is the partner of the abuser. Have they faced abuse? What can be done to reassure them? And what of the abuser? They, too, need support. What has happened in their past to cause this to happen?

Safeguarding policies give the impression that if you report abuse then that is the end of the matter. As someone who has had the misfortune to have to report such a case I know it is just the start of a very unpleasant journey. Certainly any minister directly involved in an abuse case needs much more support and protection than is currently offered, and will probably need to be relieved of normal church duties while they focus on sorting out what is a very complex and heartbreaking pastoral situation. They will also need to be assured that they would be supported pastorally and legally if the abuser were to use the disciplinary system for revenge.

This legal and technical support is not currently offered within the structures of the Methodist Church and ministers who have faced complaints have been left feeling unsupported and out in the cold. This is particularly hurtful in the reporting of abuse cases if the problem has arisen because the minister concerned has followed the Standing Orders of the Methodist Church. One way that ministers can be ensured of this legal and technical support is to join a trade union. Amicus has a 'Clergy and Church Workers' section which has supported ministers who have faced this ordeal in the past.

Training people for their new roles is vital and a number of courses are available. If you want to train children's and young people's leaders then the *Kaleidoscope*[2] course can be used. Fleggburgh (a case study church), a village church of just seven members, sent five of those members on a *Kaleidoscope* course. It was the course that gave them the confidence to choose and implement a suitable model for their children's work. There are *Kaleidoscope* tutors around the country

and your local Regional Training and Development Officer or Diocesan Youth Officer will know whom you should contact.

Having been trained it is the volunteers who are in a good position to judge which kind of model for children's work is the most suitable to the local area. Hopefully the previous chapters will have helped in this process, but it still should involve some visits to see the models in action in other churches in your locality. Such visits certainly proved helpful to Elburton (another case study church) when they were exploring what to do in the future. A look at the Family Friendly Churches Web Site may help in the process of identifying such churches.

If the chosen direction is towards all-age worship, even for the first few minutes of the service, then it is most appropriate to appoint, train and authorise a group of worship leaders. There are a number of training courses for this work.

It may be necessary to acquire equipment. Before buying equipment do look around and see what is available. For example, LCD projectors are quite common in businesses and schools these days and it may be possible for a church to borrow one at weekends.

If you intend to buy electronic equipment do look at the earlier chapter (pages 51 to 70) and the Family Friendly Web Site.

If you need to purchase capital equipment then do consider applying for grants. There may be money around if you look. My circuit, for example, has a number of Sunday school funds from churches that have closed. Methodists would be able to use money from the Circuit Advance Fund for such purchases and it is probably worth looking at the district and Connexional funds for help. They are very helpful if you have an imaginative project. There are also local grant-making bodies that might help and it is probably worth contacting your Regional Training and Development Officer. No doubt other denominations have funds for similar purposes.

Don't forget to include the costs of insurance and maintenance in your estimates.

vii) Implementation

If the work is drastically different from what you are doing at the moment or a plant of completely new work, then consider having a dry run. This was done at 'The Bridge' in Burbage. They ran a couple of their new services and members of the team setting it up came along and acted out the role of visitors. In this way they were able to check that the logistics worked, the welcome was warm and to iron out any problems before going public.

Publicity must of good quality. It must look fun and exciting, and there must be plenty of it. It is much better to put flyers into the hands of individuals, than to stick the odd poster on the church notice-board. This is where the work in the schools will really pay off. My experience is that once the relationship has been built head teachers are generally willing to distribute flyers to the children and this is by far the easiest and quickest way of getting publicity into the hands of children and their parents.

Also consider placing stories in the local media. It may be interesting to the local press that a local church has become family friendly and this would give a good opportunity for you to explain to your local community how your church is changing. There is a draft press release on the CD-ROM for you to use if you wish, along with some hints to help you to take full advantage of it.

Why not launch your project with a fun event such as a sports day followed by a barbeque? In my circuit I have also used holiday clubs to launch new work or build up existing work.

Do not expect that everyone who comes to the launch will start coming to your weekly children's group. If you are starting from scratch then work to attract children aged up to around ten. Children of this age are reasonably easy to attract into a church if the provision for them is fun, exciting and colourful. Do not expect to attract teenagers into your church from cold as this is extremely difficult, certainly for new work. I have found that the only way of building a teenage group is to build a group of 9-11 year olds and really nurture them over the next few years.

If having done all this and you have your first session and no one new comes along, be patient and hold all your plans in abeyance. If it is a Sunday morning event, keep the equipment, rota and plans there ready, for the morning will come when a family will turn up on your doorstep and you are ready to show them that your church is family friendly. This is so important. Nothing less than the long-term future of your church depends on it.

8

What about rural churches?

Those who worship in rural churches may think that all this might work for the larger town centre churches, but that many of the ideas suggested are beyond them. In my visits to the case study churches I have deliberately included a number of rural visits. These have been to show that small churches can indeed be family friendly. I have seen churches that have reversed the trend, and now families drive from the local towns to worship in these tiny village churches!

Limitations of space and resources can be more acute in a small village church, but the message from the churches I have visited is that these can be overcome.

In my own circuit there is a tiny village chapel at Wiggenhall St Germans. It had a membership of just a few elderly ladies, but they took the courageous decision to pull the pews out and replace them with chairs and a carpet. As this was done the relationship with the Anglican church in the community grew and some of the parishioners from that church came and helped in the refurbishment.

The two congregations, who worship together two Sundays a month, decided that they would like to start some work with children, particularly as the children's club run in the village hall had folded.

They decided to do this together as neither congregation had the strength to do it alone. For a week in the summer they ran a holiday club and around 15 children turned up each day. This was also done with individuals from other churches in the circuit.

A children's club now runs in the Methodist church every Wednesday evening. The two churches are still working together in the leadership of this and there is some help from individuals around the circuit. The minister and priest play an active part in this work. Good relationships are being built with the parents and there was a good represent-tation from them at an informal nativity service.

In common with other churches doing midweek children's work they are struggling to convert this to Sunday worship attendance. They are planning, and I believe other churches are doing the same, to start running a midweek all-age service once a month on a Wednesday evening.

This example illustrates two valuable points. The first is that the inflexibility that pews inflict upon a building these days can seriously restrict the work of the kingdom of God. This work would be impossible without the removal of the pews and the modernisation of the building. The second is that working ecumenically can allow churches to engage in mission that would be impossible if they were working alone.

Fleggburgh is a tiny Methodist church in rural Norfolk. It has seven members and a tiny run-down building with just one room. For example, the paint on the window frames is not peeling, it has peeled! There is no Sunday school in either the village or the circuit. The church came together and decided that they would like to embark on re-establishing children's work. Five of the seven members then went on a *Kaleidoscope* course and a tutor was sent from the next circuit.

It was quickly realised that a traditional Sunday school was not possible and so it was decided to hold all-age worship each and every Sunday. The church asked the local preachers' meeting to permit them to lead the first ten minutes and they agreed. In reality they lead for around 25 minutes and the local preacher often takes part in this time. The five who attended the course lead this part in rotation. They use the ROOTS material and they ask the local preachers to do the same. This gives the worship a sense of unity and direction.

The church is divided. On one side of the aisle are the chairs where everyone sits for the first 25 minutes. On the other side are some low tables on which work is placed for the children. In the centre is a blackboard which is used for the words of prayer. When the local preacher takes over the children move to the tables and fairly quietly get on with their work. A couple of

helpers go and sit with them, but can still participate in the service and hear the sermon as they are in the same room.

In a relatively short time a number of children, with at least one parent, have started attending the church.

The example shows that where there is a desire to be family friendly, limitations of size and personnel can be overcome. The training phase was also very important as it ensured that the correct decisions were made throughout the process.

Blackshaw Head is a tiny Methodist chapel in the hills above Hebden Bridge in Yorkshire. If you didn't know it existed you would never find it. It is tucked away on a hillside in a village that appears to have no road signs to it. The church has just three or four rows of pews filled by a number of families and children. Several families drive in from the surrounding towns into the neighbourhood. Although the church already had a Sunday school it was decided that this work should be enhanced. They decided to lead the first part of the Sunday service themselves. There was some opposition from the local preachers' meeting but the circuit ministerial staff and the Superintendent Minister were in full support. He was happy to co-operate with this and plan only those preachers who were willing to participate.

They decided to use the Living Stones[1] material which follows the Three-Year Common Lectionary and preachers are also encouraged to use this material. There is a time of worship using modern songs before the service; then the first part of the service is very child-orientated and led by a member of the local congregation if the preacher feels unsure about leading it.

They run a number of all-age services; these are always shown as 'Local Arrangements' and are led by the local congregation. They also run a quarterly 'Praise Party' which is very much along the lines of a holiday club.

This example, and that of Flegg-borough, show the importance of the congregation being very involved in the delivery of family friendly worship.

Wiveton is an Anglican church in north Norfolk. Here all age-worship is held once a month and is led by a very enthusiastic lay woman. The whole act of worship takes place in the choir stalls and a carpet is placed on the floor between them. Children are encouraged to sit on this carpet and are free to wander around as much as they wish.

Music is provided by the organist, a guitarist and a young person playing the flute. The atmosphere is warm and friendly. The songs, prayers and address are all geared to children and the service lasts for just over half an hour.

Another church in the benefice hosts a similar service on another Sunday in the month (because of the retreat of the sea, there are four Anglican churches now within walking distance of each other) and all the churches have 'children's chapels' where children can go to find books and materials on other Sundays. The service, particularly in the summer, often includes a wander around the churchyard and then finishes with a game on the village green.

This excellent work in an unpromising rural situation shows again what can be done with enthusiasm and vision.

There are areas where village churches can have an advantage. It is much easier for them to make and build links with the local community. If the village has a school then it is generally easy for members of the church or the minister/priest to make a contribution and build good connections. In a small community the word will go round quickly if good and creative work is being done. The key in all of this is visibility. Be active in the community and be seen to be active.

When families come to a village church for the first time be very careful about your expectations of them. I have spoken to families who have tried out a village church and have come away with the impression that if they went back they would be running the place in three months' time. If this impression is given then the family will almost certainly go and look elsewhere. It is not that people are unwilling to help and make a contribution, but they do need to be given a chance to settle in first.

It is also true that there is less willingness in the younger generation to serve on committees, and more willingness to serve in other, more practical ways. Do not expect the younger people who come to your church to want to fit into the structure and run the church in the ways that it has always been done.

However, a village church can offer a greater level of care and concern than large churches that struggle to find ways and structures of providing pastoral care and support for people. In general a good level of pastoral care and support is almost inherent in a village church. Try and find ways of offering this support to the families in your village – perhaps even to those who do not come to church.

A number of village churches run successful midweek clubs and are now starting to experiment with linking them to an all-age worship service also during the week. The hope is that this will draw the families of the children into, initially, a monthly act of family friendly worship.

Much of all this is about attempting to plug the church back into the community it serves. This is surely something that can be done more easily in a village than in even a small town.

9

How family friendly churches can be supported

In an earlier chapter I explored the idea of building a children's ministry on 'Fun', 'Friendship' and 'Jesus'. When I look at much of the material produced for children I see a lot of evidence for the presence of the last two but, sadly, not much for the first. Much of what is produced for children is beautifully balanced, wonderfully politically correct and often profound – but seems so dreadfully dull. I find we are short of resources that keep all these things, but also are great fun!

Our children live in a technological world. In my circuit one or two of the middle-aged preachers have developed skills and can work with PowerPoint™ and the circuit data projector. The approach of two teenagers who are on trial to be local preachers is totally different. They merely assume that this is the way to work and their skills in this area appear to be inherent.

We need a source for colourful, bright, fun resources that make use of the internet, PowerPoint™, video, computer games, MIDI-files, etc. Is it possible, for example, to produce a children's song book supplied with a disk of lively, interesting MIDI accompaniments? Not all Sunday schools have musicians these days.

We also need good resources for worship that make use of these new technologies. Most churches that use data projection are using it as a sort of slick overhead projector. This technology is capable of so much more, but we need some excellent resources for it such as animated versions of words of songs and liturgies, photographs and video clips to help prayer and meditation, children's addresses and visual aids for sermons. At the moment individuals, usually ministers, are spending hours assembling such resources. This is effort that is being duplicated around the country.

Whilst talking about technology I do worry about the way we purchase it around the circuits. The purchasing is often in the hands of people who, at best, are groping their way forward and are easy prey for ambitious salespersons. I have placed on the Family Friendly Churches Web Site a number of fact sheets to help people in purchasing technology, but I have long believed that churches should set up Technology Centres. I firmly believe that such centres could save churches many thousands of pounds and yet could be set up in such a way that they at least break even themselves. There is no doubt that churches are missing out on huge discounts that can be obtained by the bulk buying of software. My guess is also that churches are not always aware that they can also obtain a charities' discount from Microsoft and probably other vendors as well.

It might seem from the above that I feel that technology is the answer to everything. I certainly do not believe that. In terms of 'friendship' we can offer to children the quality attention of a concerned adult, and I believe that this is something quite rare and special these days. Children do seek this out and respond to it, but we do need the 'fun' to draw them to us first.

Although we have excellent resources for training lay people in children's ministry, that cannot be said of our ministers. I received very little in my own training during the early 1990s and my wife confirms that little had changed in her training in the early part of this millennium. Is it not possible, at the very least, to put ministers through the *Kaleidoscope* course whilst they are at college? It is not enough to say that it could be done while in ministry. I have tried to do this course in circuit and found the pressures were such that I attended fewer than half the sessions.

I also find it disturbing to hear newly trained ministers leaving college saying that they do not feel called to children's and young people's ministry, and this statement remaining unchallenged. I believe that to say this is no more acceptable than saying you do not feel called to elderly people's ministry – now imagine the outcry if someone was brave enough to say that!

There needs to be some kind of backing for those ministers who are prepared to walk this path and engage personally in children's and young people's ministry. It can be bumpy doing the things laid out in this book and making the changes required to make a church family friendly, such as reforming worship, starting youth groups, starting children's groups and giving time and energy to focus on all-age groups and not just exclusively on the over-70s. It has been my personal experience that far too many congregations resent rather than welcome the influx of children, young people and families. There are those within our churches who begrudge the time a minister gives to any other age group and they can make life very uncomfortable for him or her. Those ministers brave enough to tackle them need some kind of mechanism to support and protect them.

Many, if not most, of our local preachers do not feel comfortable or able to lead family friendly worship well. I think this needs the following responses:

1) Resources to encourage existing local preachers to develop skills in these areas as part of their continued and ongoing training. For example, I find that too many preachers do not know the new hymns and worship songs and do not even have the books in which they can be found. I also suspect that a lot of help is needed in sermon structure and basic communication skills.

2) There needs to be a radical reform of training for new preachers. In the courses I see, the amount of material on all-age worship is minimal. This serves to give the message that it is not really a key skill, whilst the premise of this book is the reverse. The same is true of sermon structure and communication skills. Whilst I accept that theology is important – and with a BD and Doctorate I have shown this to be true – as I have trained preachers I have come to believe that their training overvalues theology at the expense of giving them even basic communication skills.

3) There needs to be a shift in the balance of power between churches and preachers. Preachers need to be made very aware that to come and do 'your thing' to a congregation where 'your thing' is wholly inappropriate in that church is no longer acceptable, and that it is a good thing for congregations to have a house style and to participate in the construction and delivery of an act of worship. Some (many) Superintendents are already implementing such a policy by stealth by carefully manipulating the plan.

The itinerant system doesn't always help here and I think perhaps needs to be thought about. Teenagers become much attached to the minister with whom they grow up and show them a great deal of loyalty and affection. To have that person taken away from them at a critical stage in their development is devastating, and often it is very difficult for the new minister to build the same relationship with them. This is probably not enough reason to throw away the itinerancy system, but it is an issue that needs to be tackled. The answer is not an easy one, but maybe the situation of the young people could be taken seriously when considering the extension of a minister's term of office.

The other aspect that needs to be looked at is continuity from one minister to the next. There does seem to be an almost unspoken rule that if the previous minister had this style, then the next must be as close to the opposite as we can find. This does mean that at best there is no consistency from one appointment to the next, and at worst that the next minister undoes all the gains of their predecessor.

Finally, I am very concerned that many hymn books have no children's section. Although by now we would probably not be using any of the children's hymns in the book as they date very quickly, not having a children's section sends all the wrong messages about who is welcome in worship.

All of this book is a challenge to individual churches and their parent denominations. The paths laid out in this book are not easy to follow. They will demand hard work and may cause controversy, but they are worthwhile as there is nothing less than the future of the traditional churches at stake. I don't imagine for one moment that the family friendly route is the only route, but I believe fervently it offers a way to turn our churches around. In fact the only route that probably won't work is to keep on doing the same old thing in the same old way.

I urge you to look at your church and in prayer and consultation find a new way forward and go for it. If that route is the family friendly route, then you will find much in this book, CD-ROM and web site to help you, but all of this cannot equal the effect achieved when we listen to God and allow the Holy Spirit to guide and empower us.

Endnotes

1. The current situation

1. Source: The Annual and Triennial returns of the Methodist Church as published in the *Conference Directory*, Peterborough, Methodist Publishing House, 1959-2001.

2. Source: The Annual and Triennial returns of the Methodist Church as published in the *Conference Directory*, Peterborough, Methodist Publishing House, 1959-2001.

3. Source: The returns from the Methodist Churches in the East Anglia District as held in the RTDO office in Norwich. This information is not published.

4. Source: Philip Escott and Alison Gelder, *Denominational Results for The Methodist Church*, New Malden, Churches Information for Mission 2002, 2002, p. 6.

5. Figures kindly supplied by the Church of England from their Denomination Results which are yet to be published.

6. From the service of Baptism of a Young Child in *The Methodist Worship Book*, Peterborough, Methodist Publishing House, 1999, p. 72-73.

2. Churches that buck the trend

1. *Kaleidoscope*, Peterborough: Methodist Publishing House, ISBN 0 7197 0921 0.

2. David Burfield, *Worship Leaders Training Pack*, Peterborough, Methodist Publishing House, updated in 2000.

3. *Kaleidoscope*, Peterborough: Methodist Publishing House, ISBN 0 7197 0921 0.

4. Elements of all-age worship

1. This is a new computerised edition of the Bible which includes animations, encyclopaedia and virtual tours. Available from Sunrise Software, www.sunrise-software.co.uk

2. *At the Breaking of the Bread* – Standard Edition, Peterborough, Methodist Publishing House, June 2001. A quite stunning illustrated version of the Holy Communion Services from the much acclaimed *Methodist Worship Book*. The text is beautifully enhanced by illustrations from Turvey Abbey. ISBN 1 85852 208 0. 80pp. Available from the Methodist Publishing House, www.mph.org.uk

3. *The Dramatised Bible*, Michael Perry (Editor), Marshall Pickering, 1997, ISBN 0551017791.

4. Available from Sunrise Software, www.sunrise-software.co.uk

5. Using technology in worship

1. www.FamilyFriendlyChurches.org.uk

2. www.openoffice.org

3. www.sunrise-software.co.uk

4. www.dmmusic.co.uk/av

5. *Visual Liturgy* is available from the Methodist Publishing House at www.mph.org.uk

6. The Revd David Cooper, 29 Burlington Rd., Altrincham, Cheshire. W14 1HR. Email DavidCoop@btinternet.com

6. A look at the rest of the church

1. www.disability.gov.uk/index

2. www.worldaction.info

7. Bringing about the changes

1. *Safeguarding – A policy for good practice in the care of children and young people*, Peterborough: Methodist Publishing House, April 2003, ISBN 1 85852 246 3.

2. *Kaleidoscope*, Peterborough: Methodist Publishing House, revised 1998, ISBN 0 7197 0921 0.

8. What about rural churches?

1. Susan Sayers, *Living Stones: A Year*, Stowmarket, Kevin Mayhew, 1998, ISBN: 184003212X. There is one book for each year of the lectionary.

Appendix

Resources

The Family Friendly Charter

Suggested Mission Statement: <Insert name of Church> aims to be a community where all people are welcomed regardless of age, gender, race, ability and background to meet to worship God and to be encouraged to deepen their Christian discipleship.

The Charter itself

At <Insert name of Church> we express the love of God for us and our love for each other by working towards becoming a place where:

1) All people are welcomed to worship God with us regardless of age, gender, race, ability and background.

   We accept that not everyone whom we welcome will have the same understanding of worship as we do. We as a church will undertake to develop ways of broadening worship to satisfy the needs of a wider community. We understand that in such a community we cannot expect every element in every act of worship to be in a style that we as individuals would personally like it to be. We also understand that in this charter we are extending a welcome to those who may not always be able to meet our personal expectations of conduct. We will accept such situations with understanding and good grace.

2) We will encourage all those who are part of this community to grow in their Christian understanding and discipleship.

   We accept that none of us has all the answers and so we will journey together to grow in our understanding of what it means to be Christian. We will give teaching and encouragement to all our community regardless of where they are in their journey. We will accept the insights of all members of our community as part of our communal understanding of who God is. We will help and support parents in the difficult task of bringing up children in the Christian faith. We will explore what discipleship means for us in our wider community and put this into practice.

3) We will provide facilities that will make our premises and practices accessible to all.

   We will work to remove any barriers (physical, mental or spiritual) that prevent others from joining the full life of this community. This may mean changing some elements of our building or practices that we may treasure, but we will accept this with understanding and good grace. We will provide special facilities particularly to help children and those with disabilities.

4) We will do all in our power to ensure that all members of our community are kept safe from harm.

We understand that this means that we must take seriously the requirements placed on us by the law to protect children from those who would harm them. We must be careful not to exploit those who are physically, mentally or spiritually vulnerable. We must constantly be vigilant to keep our premises as safe a place as possible.

Resources and links to web sites

These also appear on the Family Friendly Churches Web Site.

For information about using puppets take a look at 'One Way UK Creative Ministries' on <http://www.onewayuk.com>, 'Hands up for God' on <http://www.dldoyle.freeserve.co.uk> and 'Puppet Resources' on <http://www.puppetresources.com>.

For information and scripts for dramas check out: 'Lifelines Drama Group' on <http://www.lifelines.org.uk/drama> and 'CURTAINS!' on <http://www.ed2ed.freeserve.co.uk/cchurch/curtains/default.htm>.

Both of these sites have sketches available and links to other sites.

There are a number of professional Christian drama groups around. The best known are Riding Lights on <http://www.ridinglights.org>, the Lantern Arts Centre at <http://www.lanternarts.org>, the Rascal Theatre Company and the work done by the Jasperian Theatre Company.

Contents of the CD-ROM

To run the CD-ROM in the CD or DVD drive of your machine it should load automatically. On the CD-ROM you should find:

1. Copies of the Family Friendly Charter in HTML, Word and PowerPoint™ format.

2. Ten action points from the case studies in HTML, Word and PowerPoint™ format.

3. Case Studies for each of the churches visited during the research for this book in HTML and PowerPoint™ format.

4. PowerPoint™ presentation of Chapter 1 to be used in Church Councils.

5. The words of the liturgy of *The Methodist Worship Book*, coupled with the illustrations from Turvey Abbey – for the Christmas services.

6. Words of popular carols (out of copyright) with the Turvey Abbey backgrounds and images.

7. Words of around 100 out of copyright popular hymns from *Hymns & Psalms* with my own photographs, backgrounds etc.

8. Lively MIDI instrumentations of the same hymns.

9. The Burbage survey form – courtesy of Peter Hancock.

10. Draft press release.